A JOURNEY OF RICHES

Elevating Your Life

10 Stories to Empower Your Soul

To Alison + Gerry
Thank you for being part of my journey of riches.
Rebecca x x

A Journey of Riches – Elevating Your Life
10 Stories to Empower Your Soul

Published by Motion Media International
Editors: Eric Wyman, Yasmin Phillip, Parker Hansen, Rosemary Lawton and Arynne Priest
Cover Design: Motion Media International
Typesetting & Assembly: Motion Media International

Printing: Amazon and Ingram Sparks
Creator: John Spender - Primary Author
Title: *A Journey of Riches – Elevating Your Life*

ISBN Digital: 978-1-925919-75-2
ISBN Print: 978-1-925919-76-9
Subjects: Motivation, Inspiration, Memoir

ACKNOWLEDGMENTS

Reading and writing are gifts that very few give to themselves. It is such a powerful way to reflect and gain closure from the past; reading and writing are therapeutic processes. The experience raises one's self-esteem, confidence, and awareness of self.

I learned this when I collated the first book in the *A Journey of Riches* series, which now includes thirty-four books with over 300 co-authors from over 40 countries. Writing about your personal experiences is difficult, and I honor and respect every author who has collaborated in the series.

For many authors, English is their second language, a significant achievement. In creating this anthology of short stories, I have been touched by the generosity, gratitude, and shared energy this experience has given everyone.

The inspiration for *A Journey of Riches, Elevating Your Life* was born from my desire to share empowering stories to unleash your inner strength. Each chapter is written by a different author sharing their wisdom on creating the resilience in finding their inner strength.

I want to thank all the authors for entrusting me with their unique memories, encounters, and wisdom. Thank you for sharing and opening the door to your soul so others may learn from your experience. I trust the readers will gain confidence from your successes and wisdom from your failures.

I also want to thank my family. I know you are proud of me, seeing how far I have come from that ten-year-old boy learning to read and write at a basic level. So big shout out to Mom, Robert, Dad, and Merril; my brother Adam and his daughter Krystal; my sister Hollie and her partner Brian; my nephew Charlie and niece, Heidi; thank you for your support. Also, kudos to my grandparents, Gran, and Pop, who are alive and well, and Ma and Pa, who now rest in peace. They accept me just as I am with all my travels and adventures worldwide.

Thanks to the team at Motion Media International; you have done an excellent job editing and collating this book. It was a pleasure working with you on this successful project, and I thank you for your patience in dealing with the changes and adjustments along the way.

Thank you, the reader, for having the courage to look at your life and how you can improve your future in a fast and rapidly changing world.

Again, thank you to my co-authors: Alessandro Gavello, Amita McBride, Colleen Sabol-Olitsky, Gabriela D Delgadillo, Idaliz Romero, Lynn Hayward, Mariese B Vacalares, Rebecca Shannon and Sharee Siva.

With gratitude,
John Spender

Table of Contents

Praise for *A Journey of Riches Book Series*

"The *A Journey of Riches* book series is a great collection of inspiring short stories that will leave you wanting more!"
~ Alex Hoffmann, Network Marketing Guru.

"If you are looking for an inspiring read to get you through any change, this is it! This book comprises many gripping perspectives from a collection of successful international authors with a tone of wisdom to share."
~ Theera Phetmalaigul, Entrepreneur/Investor.

"*A Journey of Riches* is an empowering series that implements two simple words in overcoming life's struggles.

By diving into the meaning of the words 'problem' and 'challenge,' you will be motivated to believe in the triumph of perseverance. With many different authors from all around the world coming together to share various stories of life's trials, you will find yourself drenched in encouragement to push through even the darkest of battles. The stories are heartfelt personal shares of moving through and transforming challenges into rich life experiences.

The book will move, touch, and inspire your spirit to face and overcome life's adversities. It is a truly inspirational read. Thank you for being the kind, open soul you are, John!"
~ Casey Plouffe, Seven Figure Network Marketer.

"A must-read for anyone facing major changes or challenges in life right now. This book will give you the courage to overcome any struggle with confidence, grace, and ease."
~ Jo-Anne Irwin, Transformational Coach, and Best-Selling Author.

"I have enjoyed the *Journey of Riches* book series. Each person's story is written from the heart, and everyone's journey is different. However, we all have a story to tell, and John Spender does an amazing job of finding authors and combining their stories into uplifting books."
~ Liz Misner Palmer, Foreign Service Officer.

"A timely read as I'm facing a few challenges right now. I like the various insights from the different authors. This book will inspire you to move through any challenge or change you are experiencing."
~ David Ostrand, Business Owner.

"I've known John Spender for a while now, and I was blessed with an opportunity to be in book four in the series. I know that you will enjoy this new journey, like the rest of the books in the series. The collection of stories will assist you with making changes, dealing with challenges, and seeing that transformation is possible for your life."
~ Charlie O'Shea, Entrepreneur.

"*A Journey of Riches* series will draw you in and help you dig deep into your soul. These authors have unbelievable life stories of purpose inside of them. John Spender is dedicated to bringing peace, love, and adventure to the world of his readers! Dive into this series, and you will be transformed!"
~ Jeana Matichak, Author of *Finding Peace*.

"Awesome! Truly inspirational! It is amazing what the human spirit can achieve and overcome! Highly recommended!"
~ Fabrice Beliard, Australian Business Coach and Best-Selling Author.

"*A Journey of Riches* Series is a must-read. It is an empowering collection of inspirational and moving stories full of courage, strength, and heart. Bringing peace and awareness to those lucky enough to read to assist and inspire them on their life journey."
~ Gemma Castiglia, Avalon Healing, Best Selling Author.

"The *A Journey of Riches* book series is an inspirational collection of books that will empower you to take on any challenge or change in life."
~ Kay Newton, Midlife Stress Buster, and Best-Selling Author.

"*A Journey of Riches* book series is an inspiring collection of stories, sharing many different ideas and perspectives on how to overcome challenges, deal with change and make empowering choices in your life. Open the book anywhere and let your mood choose where you need to read. Buy one of the books today; you'll be glad that you did!"
~ Trish Rock, Modern Day Intuitive, Best-Selling Author, Speaker, Psychic & Holistic Coach.

"*A Journey of Riches* is another inspiring read. The authors are from all over the world, and each has a unique perspective to share that will have you thinking differently about your current circumstances in life. An insightful read!"
~ Alexandria Calamel, Success Coach and Best-Selling Author.

"The *A Journey of Riches* book series is a collection of real-life stories, which are truly inspiring and give you the confidence that no matter what you are dealing with in your life, there is a light at the end of the tunnel and a very bright one at that. Totally empowering!"
~ John Abbott, Freedom Entrepreneur.

"An amazing collection of true stories from individuals who have overcome great changes, and who have transformed their lives and used their experience to uplift, inspire and support others."
~ Carol Williams, Author, Speaker & Coach.

"You can empower yourself from the power within this book that can help awaken the sleeping giant within you. John has a purpose in life to bring inspiring people together to share their wisdom for the benefit of all who venture deep into this book series. If you are looking for inspiration to be someone special, this book can be your guide."
~ Bill Bilwani, Renowned Melbourne Restaurateur.

"In the *A Journey of Riches* series, you will catch the impulse to step up, reconsider and settle for only the very best for yourself and those around you. Penned from the heart and with an unflinching drive to make a difference for the good of all, *A Journey of Riches* series is must-read."
~ Steve Coleman, author of *Decisions, Decisions! How to Make the Right One Every Time.*

"Do you want to be on top of your game? *A Journey of Riches* is a must-read with breakthrough insights that will help you do just that!" ~ Christopher Chen, Entrepreneur.

"In *A Journey of Riches*, you will find the insight, resources, and tools you need to transform your life. By reading the author's stories, you, too, can be inspired to achieve your greatest accomplishments and what is truly possible for you. Reading this book activates your true potential for transforming your life way beyond what you think is possible. Read it and learn how you, too, can have a magical life."
~ Elaine Mc Guinness, Best Selling Author of *Unleash Your Authentic Self!*

"If you are looking for an inspiring read, look no further than the *A Journey of Riches* book series. The books are an inspiring collection of short stories that will encourage you to embrace life even more. I highly recommend you read one of the books today!"
~ Kara Dono, Doula, Healer, and Best-Selling Author.

"The *A Journey of Riches* book series is filled with real-life short stories of heartfelt tribulations turned into uplifting self-transformation by the power of the human spirit to overcome adversity. The journeys captured in these books will encourage you to embrace life in a whole new way. I highly recommend reading this inspiring anthology series."
~ Chris Drabenstott, Best Selling Author and Editor.

"There is so much motivational power in the *A Journey of Riches* series!! Each book is a compilation of inspiring, real-life stories by several different authors, which makes the journey feel more relatable and success more attainable. If you are looking for something to move you forward, you'll find it in one (or all) of these books."
~ Cary MacArthur, Personal Empowerment Coach.

"I've been fortunate to write with John Spender, and now, I call him a friend. *A Journey of Riches* book series features real stories that have inspired me and will inspire you. John has a passion for finding amazing people from all over the world, giving the series a global perspective on relevant subject matters."
~ Mike Campbell, Fat Guy Diary, LLC.

"The *A Journey of Riches* series is the reflection of beautiful souls who have discovered the fire within. Each story takes you inside the truth of what truly matters in life. While reading these stories, my heart space expanded to understand that our most significant contribution in this lifetime is to give and receive love. May you also feel inspired as you read this book."
~ Katie Neubaum, Author of *Transformation Calling*.

"*A Journey of Riches* is an inspiring testament that love and gratitude are the secret ingredients to living a happy and fulfilling life. This series is sure to inspire and bless your life in a big way. Truly an inspirational read that is written and created by real people, sharing real-life stories about the power and courage of the human spirit."
~ Jen Valadez, Emotional Intuitive and Best-Selling Author.

"If you are looking for an inspirational read, look no further than the *A Journey of Riches* book series. The books are an inspiring and educational collection of short stories from the author's soul that will encourage you to embrace life even more. I've even given them to my clients, too, so that their journeys inspire them in life for wealth, health, and everything else in between. I recommend you make it a priority to read one of the books today!"
~ Goro Gupta, Chief Education Officer, Mortgage Terminator, Property Mentor.

PREFACE

I collated this book and chose authors from around the world to share their experiences about what "Elevating Your Life" meant to them. This book is the collective wisdom of the various authors' journeys to unleash their inner strength. This eclectic collection of chapters encompasses many different writing styles and perspectives that embrace the intelligence of our hearts and intuition.

Like all of us, each author has a unique story and insight to share with you. One or more authors might have lived through an experience like one in your life. Their words could be just what you need to read to help you through your challenges and motivate you to continue on your chosen path.

Storytelling has been how humankind has communicated ideas and learning throughout our civilization. While we have become more sophisticated with technology and life in the modern world is now more convenient, there is still much discontent and dissatisfaction. Many people have also moved away from reading books and are missing valuable information that could help them move forward with a positive outlook. Moving toward the tasks or dreams that scare us breeds confidence in growing towards becoming better versions of ourselves.

I think it is essential to turn off the television, slow down, read, reflect, and take the time to appreciate everything you have in life. Start with an anthology book as they offer a cornucopia of viewpoints relating to a particular theme. Here, it's fear and how others have dealt with it. We feel stuck in life or have challenges in a particular area because we see the problem through the same lens that created it. With this compendium and all the books in the *A Journey of Riches* series, you have many writing styles and perspectives that will help you think and see your challenges differently, motivating you to elevate your circumstances.

Anthology books are also great because you can start from any chapter and gain valuable insight or a nugget of wisdom without the feeling you have missed something from the earlier episodes.

I love reading many personal development books because learning and personal growth are vital. If you are not learning and growing, you're staying the same. Everything in the universe is growing, expanding, and changing. If we are not open to different ideas and ways to think and be, then even the most skilled and educated can become close-minded.

This book series aims to open you up to diverse ways of perceiving your reality. It encourages and gives you many avenues of thinking about the same subject. I wish for you to feel empowered to make a decision that will best suit you in moving forward with your life. As Albert Einstein said, **"We cannot solve problems with the same level of thinking that created them."** So, with Einstein's words in mind, let your mood pick a chapter, or read from the beginning to the end and be guided to find the answers you seek.

With gratitude,
John Spender

"Keep your face always toward the sunshine - and shadows will fall behind you."

~ Walt Whitman

CHAPTER ONE

Grace and The Phoenix

By Amita McBride

The tiny plane lurched and bounced as it climbed up through the clouds. The ground below fell away like a watercolor in the rain. As I sat clutching my knees closely to my chest, I listened to the deafening roar of the engine while my heart raced. It reminded me of the children's story about "The Little Engine That Could." It's little engines burning with the effort of going higher and higher over the Alps. Sitting on the floor of this tiny plane, the vibrations were so intense, it felt like the bolts were going to come loose and… Holy mother of God, is that duct tape? I needed to get a grip, so like a mantra, I repeated quietly to myself over and over: "Amita, breathe, breathe, slowly, calmly, breathe. This is an amazing opportunity to face your fears while fulfilling your promise."

I had always wondered why someone would want to throw themselves out of a perfectly good airplane. But now I was one of those people! I did not realize at the time that while this adventure was on the spectrum of the terrifying, it was also about to become a huge gift for my heart and soul as well.

It wasn't until my companion, my literal lifeline of no more than twenty-plus years, reached over my shoulder and asked, "Are you ready?" while grinning from ear to ear, like we were out on a casual stroll for ice cream, that I was overcome with the immense desire to knock that smile right off his sweet face.

"Noooo" squeaked its way out of my throat while I attempted a contracted smile back his way. He edged forward and began clipping himself to my vest—a tandem jump. Was I insane? What was I doing? I am terrified of heights, complete with full-on vertigo. You know, the kind that wraps itself insidiously around and through you, leaning you ever more precariously toward any outcropping you are in the vicinity of. Yeah, That kind!

As he opened the door of the tiny plane, my perspective took an instant and incredulous flip. Just a wee moment before and on the verge of hyperventilating, I was wondering if this plane was actually going to get us to altitude or if it was moments away from vibrating apart with all the bits and pieces plummeting out of the sky, including us. Now, the small plane felt like the safest place on Earth, in the heavens, anywhere!

I wanted to wrap my arms and legs around the wing attachment like a sloth. Like the sloth I had worked with in the Baltimore Aquarium who refused to eat the peas, I attempted to hide in every sort of delectable morsel of food you can imagine. Perched high in the treetops, he hung upside down with his three toes wrapped around my wrist, gazing at me with a Yoda-like expression, all while squeezing my wrist ever so tightly when he suspected a pea was headed his way. He was so charming about it all while making it VERY clear he wasn't having any of it. Well, I was pretty darn close to grabbing the heck out of that plane wing in the same freaking way.

I was strapped to a man I barely knew; wait, what was his name again? Having signed papers that said the company was not responsible for my death, injury, or all other manner of horrifying prospects, he gave me the thumbs up and began inching me towards the open door of the tiny craft. I tried to say I had changed my mind, but the noise was so all-encompassing that he could not hear me. "Come on, Amita, find your Moxie!" (Moxie is my nickname, by the way).

As he edged me out onto the wing of the plane, the last few fibers of my being almost disintegrated into dust."Oh my god!" BREATHE. A promise to my son to take him skydiving. That is what started this whole shebang. He was no longer in this world, so I was not beholden to this promise anymore, was I? Yet something deep within me was tugging at me to take him skydiving. Or was it, in fact, him taking me? What was the real Universal plan unfolding here?

With goggles strapped on so tightly, my face took on the appearance of a puffer fish. I did my best to smile. "Oh no, I think I need the bathroom. Please, please, please do not add that to this already fraught experience," I pleaded to myself. I would have to move states. The horror… "Okay, breathe, Amita, breathe."

Did I mention I have an incredible fear of heights? As we perched precariously on the edge of the open door with the wind whipping mercilessly at our bodies, I tried again to tell him I really had changed my mind, but my words were carried helplessly away into the void, probably bouncing off of some unsuspecting bird hundreds of feet below.

As he threw another one of those ridiculously excited smiles my way, he simultaneously launched us out of the aircraft and into the air. I will not repeat here the expletives that poured from my mouth like a torrent as the sky took us into her bosom.

IT WAS MIRACULOUS! I transcended the moment. It was incredible, phenomenal, and unlike any experience I have ever had. It was in it's own category. I was free, one with the universe, the sky, myself, and life. Weightless, moving at such speed through such density, the air particles, the quantum field parting, making way yet fully supporting our free fall through time and space. It was extraordinary.

My only prayer to the universe had been for me not to be injured. If I died, so be it, as this was a risky business indeed, just not injured. I had suffered enough already, and this sojourn was an act of deep love and courage. Little did I know how much it was going to elevate my life, to reset me, to fill every cell, photon, and telomere in my body with so much life, such high vibrational energy that so much condensed grief was going to be literally sucked out of me and carried away into the heavens.

It was incredible! From this vantage point, the cliffs along the Colorado River in Glenwood Springs were mind-blowing. Yellow rafts were floating in the river with teeny tiny people in them. The sunlight was so brilliant, reflecting off of everything! My heart was wide open, and I cried with the beauty, my bravery, the gift, for my son, for everything. The clouds, the endless horizon - oh, how the eagles see all so clearly. I felt free, fear had no hold here, ripped away by the sheer velocity of being in the absolute NOW present moment.

It was not until he pulled the parachute and we lurched upward with such force, sending my stomach firmly into my throat, that I began screaming, "I'M SCARED, I'M SCARED!" over and over for a good minute until we both could calm me down. It was fascinating that while free falling, the fear was gone, replaced by awe and wonder, the closest thing to flying.

But when I was brought vertical and could see my legs and feet hanging suspended in the air a couple of thousand feet up, held solely by a piece of material over our heads, while completely at the mercy of the wind and the skill of the young man strapped to me, I felt a vulnerability of such a profound nature, I was temporarily in a state of terror. That state began peeling away as I pulled my focus back onto my breathing. With my fabulous lifeline joyfully taking selfies and videos of us and our surroundings, I relaxed once more.

In awe of our magnificent Earth, mixed with the salty tears of gratitude blurring my vision and fogging up my goggles, a deeper surrender, and an even deeper presence of being and trust-filled me. Something I hadn't felt in a long time. My prayer was heard and my beloved child was indeed there with me as we floated down to earth. Well, float is a bit of an exaggeration. While we were at the mercy of the tide, carried hither and thither towards the earth would be more accurate.

As the ground began rising up to meet us, manipulating the parachute to control our speed became trickier. Our landing was about as graceful as watching an albatross attempting to land in a goat pen. My guy was amazing. The wind was strong. We left a wake behind us in all directions consisting of dirt, pebbles, and grass.

Filling my eyes, nose, ears, hair, shoes, pants, well, every crevice it could be flung into, I sat stunned for a second, feeling the ground solidly beneath my bones. I was alive and unharmed! I did it! I really did it! I faced one of my greatest fears and fulfilled my promise to take my son skydiving. Though he was safely stowed in my pocket, his ashes in a sterling silver necklace, a promise is a promise!

I was vibrating with such force that every cell of my body was wildly alert, aware, and awake! The colors were brighter, everything echoing all around me and within me. My skydiving pal told me I was the first person who was scared once the parachute was pulled and fine without it. He said that was a first in the company log!

I stayed in this state for quite some time, only returning to a calmer equilibrium days later. Still feeling deeply reset and alive in a new way, I decided to book a trip to Italy to breathe in new life and give some love to my battered being. While living in a gorgeous village, an Italian cooking course felt like the right medicine. Following it up with renting a little car, traveling, and filling my bucket with whatever presented itself, all while eating amazing food and drinking fabulous wine made my heart smile! Another daring adventure on the immediate horizon…

I had grown up flying with my father, who was a private pilot, flying us as a family in an assortment of amazing little planes, and as time passed larger planes were added to our travels. I had always stayed inside the aircrafts, so flinging myself out of one was a very different experience.

My Father also flew glider planes when I was younger. I fondly remember being towed in a glider off the edge of a cliff and pushing the red button for the cable release to our tow plane. The silence and majesty of gliding, finding a thermal, and being carried higher and higher like a bird has stayed with me all these years.

It is effortless within a thermal. It's a lot like being in the flow with trust and grace versus pushing against the current and clinging to the bank, I would surmise. Two red-tailed hawks joined us in the same thermal, fascinated by what kind of large white bird we were, and rose with us, peering into the cockpit as we climbed effortlessly within the winds of time. Gliding over meadows full of cows and quietly looking across the horizon, we slowly returned to earth, landing gently in a field while we awaited our pickup crew.

The invisible world is the real world, the manifest world. Our belief systems, thoughts, words, actions, and attitudes create our reality. It is so easy to forget that everyone else is also doing or not doing this and we are all here mushed together with our feelings, dreams, intentions, imperfections, and freak-outs.

We are not our experiences. We are not our beliefs. However, they rule how we live. We are creatures of habit, and changing those habits involves commitment and dedication. We create a platform that either holds us contracted and controlled and living in a fear-based reality or expanded, brave, and unwilling to shortchange ourselves and our dreams for any reason.

This is where self-love enters stage left as a key player. Sometimes, we go through things that literally take the ground out from under us, leaving us vulnerable, lost, and scared. It takes time and gentleness, trust and courage, and believing that life is unfolding for our highest, even if we do not understand at the time, sometimes not until years later. Sometimes, we get in our way so completely we can't see the forest for the trees. And sometimes, we just need to curl up deeply until healing and grace can find us.

The other key player entering stage right is energy. Learning how to sustain our vibration and sustainably receive blessings from the Universe and our higher manifest self is crucial. Just like a muscle, it must be worked and practiced to maintain it. Then the Phoenix finds us and blasts us into oblivion, 'poof' and we rise anew wondering what the heck we are meant to do next.

Elevating your life is not a once-in-a-lifetime event. It is the continual evolution of who you are into higher, better versions of yourself. It is amazing how easily we can focus on things outside of ourselves while procrastinating within ourselves. True transformation starts to unfold once we commit to transmuting and sloughing off the old limitations.

By opening up the protective personality with a can opener and being careful not to throw the contents all over the place, we can respectfully and reverently empty the can bit by bit to look at everything packed in there. What we can discover is pretty amazing.

It is not about tearing yourself apart. It's about observing and being curious to look at where we are most critical of ourselves, where we are too lenient, where we make excuses, sabotage ourselves, and blame others for our woes.

It is about removing all the stuff that just doesn't serve us anymore, making room for the new and giving some breathing room for our rockin' selves to stretch and explore uncharted territory. The only way to elevate your life is by committing to an authentic one, one you consistently feed and nurture because it is your life!

Initially, some things may go a bit sideways. You are overturning the apple cart, after all. Like hiking to a beautiful pristine mountain pond that draws your sweaty and weary body into its cool and refreshing waters. As you joyfully plunge in and go to stand up to wave at your friend chillin' on the shore, you suddenly find yourself sinking up to your kneecaps in foul-smelling, squishy stuff.

As it floats up all around you, the peaceful scene changes radically, and your priority now becomes evacuating the pond as quickly as possible. Initially, when you decide to upgrade your life, you may find yourself topsy-turvy.

We don't have a road map when we enter uncharted territory. That's the point! We need to move out of our comfort zone and see what we are made of and who we are under the gunk. It is your new platform, your road less traveled, to shine your light and bring your greatness into the world.

As we delve deeper, it is not that it gets harder; rather, it gets more vulnerable because we reach more of the places within us that we left behind. The mind will try anything to pull your attention away from your task. Things like "Gosh, I wonder if my toaster sold on the marketplace yet?" or "Wow, I should change the cat litter," and "I really need a new toothbrush!"

When we can be with the parts of us that have been locked away and held our hardest moments and truly love them as you would a small child or a wounded squirrel, they start to soften and dissipate and you begin to gain new perspective and insights.

Your horizon broadens and you see more clearly, with less prejudice toward yourself and others. Now there are some things in life that just plain suck and are not in the realm of bettering oneself. However, even in those circumstances, there are always choices in how you move forward. How can those experiences help you find the strength you didn't know you had to help others, create something you may not have otherwise, and so on? The list of possibilities is endless.

The time it has taken me to reconfigure myself and step forward again into the world after losing my only child, Sam, has been vast. To then also lose my only sibling, my sister, who fought cancer valiantly and left behind my two nephews, adds the tragic into tragedy. I am a mother without my precious son and now my nephews are children without a mother.

Nothing makes this scenario okay, ever. It's a lot for one little family to experience. There have been other losses and hardships as well, but the point here is that the love between my nephews and me, our reconnection, is precious, especially since there had been a rift between my sister and me for many years.

Having a year and a half with her, caring for her, rebuilding as we could, laughing and crying with her, as I am now writing these words, has been enormous. The healing that transpired, the gifts within the absolute heartbreak, are pure gold. A dear friend wrote to me while I was caring for my sister and told me about the Japanese art of Kintsugi.

She told me that when a pot breaks, they use gold mixed with lacquer to put it back together, making the broken areas even stronger and more beautiful than before. She told me she saw me that way, and needless to say, I cried and cried.

Buying my home in Montana felt like a dream, a new beginning. I was stepping forward again into life. I needed a new state, a new place, a fresh slate. I had worked in Glacier National Park many years earlier, so I knew Montana was a breathtakingly beautiful state. I was given the name of a realtor and got to know him over phone calls between Colorado and Montana. He is a fifth-generation Montanan local, a salt-of-the-earth kind of guy.

He lives in a beautiful canyon outside of Missoula where I now also reside! He told me about a special place he thought may be going on the market. He knew the couple, which led to conversations with the owners, sharing that he felt I was the right person for this unique and remarkable place. A video or two later and the result was a sale… To me!

To show how clearly we know when the universe is working in our favor, I had felt deeply the two years before to bust my buns on my little place in Colorado, which I did, and then Covid hit. People were leaving the big cities and my place was ten acres, a quarter of a mile from a reservoir. I doubled my money and walked away with the exact amount my new place cost to the penny.

I listened to my intuition, and it paid off. It was not all fun and games as I drained my savings and went through two corrupt contractors. One of whom stole a lot of money without doing the work and is still at large with multiple warrants for his arrest! The closer I got to my goal, the tougher things got, seriously testing my resolve. It is not always this way when we make changes, but I was breaking out of old stuff, so the muck was deeper.

Pulling into my new home at 10 p.m. on a hot July evening, a home I had never seen in person, I was beside myself to see it. The drive was beautiful, the canyon incredible, and I was ready to be there. With a convoy of U-Hauls, critters, vehicles, and my life, I met my realtor for the first time. He was playing basketball. Wait, what? A basketball court? I have a basketball court!! Holy Toledo!

Walking into my home elicited deep emotion through every pore of my body. An arduous 18-hour drive in crazy heat after deciding to leave my beloved Colorado was a huge decision. A maze of beautiful wood and stone and a Japanese soaking tub in the hallway built into an alcove so you could look up through the skylights and watch the moon.

Really? This is my home? I wondered if I deserved this magical place in this incredible canyon on land so quiet and beautiful. A stunning loft off the kitchen with a tree as a railing and huge windows to capture the sun's warmth add even more artistic creativity to this already magnificent design.

Imagine my surprise when, not long after moving in, I began not to feel very well. My older cat was having the same symptoms. I pressed on unpacking, hanging my art, blessing the land, the house, the trees, weed whacking the neglected land, and the roof! I have a living roof and to my immense joy, it is often visited by wild turkeys and deer with their young as they nestle in for the evening, safe from predators. Creating like crazy, flowers and plants flowing everywhere, loving into every nook and cranny.

Then the skylights began leaking, all of them. Water ran down various places on the walls and the front windows, and I was getting sicker, really sick. What was wrong with me? My Amazon plant knowledge, exercise, meditation, and intention kept me going, but it was getting really serious. I had my home inspected, and in return, I was handed a 52-page report. It can't be the house?!

Jumping forward in time, it was the house. She had been built with such care and love. Over the 40 years since she had been rooted into the earth, some had cut corners along the way. Thick rubber laid on the flat roof pushed moisture through the solid concrete walls until black mold grew behind the plaster in the old bathroom, mouse condos anywhere there were wood walls and most shockingly of all, loose fiberglass stuffed into the open ductwork of the heating system, so I was breathing in raw fiberglass.

It was everywhere! In my eyes, my throat, my lungs! It caused rashes, painful breathing, serious stuff. I felt like I was close to dying and made sure my will was in order. It even took my older cat's life. I was devastated. A coyote took one of my other cats and one of my dogs had to be put down. Jesus, Mary, and Joseph, what had I done to deserve all of this after all I had gone through to get here? This was supposed to be a new start!

I had to move back out immediately; the contractor involved is another story entirely. The stress was extreme. I didn't know anyone and my hair was falling out from the toxins and the severity of the entire situation.

What does any of this have to do with elevating your life?

EVERYTHING

A year and a half later, I am alive as I sit at my computer writing this story. I did not give up; sell and return to Colorado. I had no idea where the money would come from, but it has shown up at critical moments in remarkable ways. The house was torn down to the concrete walls, the moldy areas remediated, and a clean slate began, putting her back together and honoring her and her remarkable design. I am clearing the last remaining toxins from my sweet body with my healing protocol and support from other practitioners. The sun is beginning to shine again. I am building a whole new life, after all. The phoenix has visited often during this process.

I could look at this chain of events in many different ways. I chose to look at the hidden gifts that presented themselves throughout this time frame, even when I could not see or feel them. It propelled me into a deeper transformation. It also allowed for members of my soul tribe to come in. Wonderful guys who are completing my home with skill, deep care, and fair prices. We have become good friends and they have my back. If my old furnace had not died, the fiberglass would not have been found and I very well could have died.

I joined several different year-long courses, something I would not have been drawn to without being in such a deep state of healing. They are powerful and enriching, expanding and supporting my protocol for well-being and personal evolution.

I also joined a small mentor group offered by a man I had known many years before. There were a handful of us, and I have become dear friends with one, a doctor, who has been paramount in helping me via homeopathy, energy codes, and other resources. Another member from Australia reached out and we forged a friendship.

She is the one who connected me to "A Journey of Riches" and John Spender! Remarkable, is it not? There are many gifts of grace shining through the challenges. I have interviews coming in, an offer to be a practitioner at a beautiful healing center, new books, and so forth. I have added additional tools to my repertoire for helping others heal from exposure to such unpleasant bedfellows.

Throughout this same time frame, I had to go back to Durango and have one more surgery for abdominal adhesions. This was crazy! I was definitely going to read the fine print before incarnating again. I can see myself saying, "Oh yes, no problem at all! Add that to the list. I got this, easy peasy."

We have spoken about co-creating podcasts to help women heal their inner wounds and understand the connection between physical and emotional issues. This is powerful stuff!

Before I arrived in Montana, I had visions of a healing center and my soulmate standing next to me in front of the fireplace with good friends milling about. The first time I walked into my new home and saw the fireplace where the vision took place, my jaw dropped.

The yurt is almost complete, and an incredible greenhouse and new garden area are underway. Bees are arriving in May. Everything is coming closer to fruition.

This journey, among others, has been a massive leap of faith. I am aligning with myself in ways I never have before, even before losing my son. Even when my healing work, travels, and speaking engagements were rocking it, I still sabotaged myself, not truly believing that I deserved good relationships, love, and happiness. I felt I had to work harder than anyone else for less. Our beliefs and subconscious platforms call the shots.

Elevating your life is a journey that continues until the day you drop your body and go home. Grace glides silently alongside the Phoenix. Open and observe everything in your life with curiosity, and focus on loving yourself more than you knew you could. You will begin to heal in ways you didn't even realize you needed.

Your language changes, the way you think, the people you attract, and you do not need external approval in the same way. Your amazing, magnificent self knows which way to go because you listen to your heart and inner wisdom with conviction, knowing the Universe has your back.

The "Invictus" poem by William Ernest Henley (1875) comes to mind. If you have never read it, it will move through you like a hot fire.

This unique, beautiful home, land, and I are mirrors of one another in our journey to wholeness. She is radiant and alive and here to hold healing space for those seeking their way back into their authentic, elevated selves. I will be smiling and radiating right alongside, just like my joyful skydiving buddy.

It is our duty to achieve our sole purpose and share our specific divine gifts with humanity. This is why we are here: to elevate our consciousness and lives, to achieve our highest potential while radiating gratitude and love into the world.

Love heals when she is given with pure intention. When she is allowed within to softly nourish the sad and battered places, tenderness and grace can then take root and grow.

Big Beings Go Through Big Evolutions

Do you have the courage to love yourself that much? To do what is required to bring your authentic self into a beautiful world that awaits you? Are you living your purpose, or is it a shadow etched on the far horizon?

Imagine if we could truly master ourselves to the point of sustaining our true nature, honoring the gift of life, and deeply knowing that every action and intention we carry impacts the collective and all of life on earth.

We are falling through space and time
held by a profoundly delicate
yet resilient body suit

For our flame, our light to experience
the freedom
the unbounded expansion
of free fall
is like going home

Without weight or structure
we are held within the threads of vulnerability
through our
complete connection to all of life
within a world
where we define ourselves

Though
who we are
is defined by nothing in this world
and
always free to fly.

"Elevate yourself by elevating your mind above the chaos. Take time to be still."

~ Kevin Hall

CHAPTER TWO

Connect Thoughts to Action

By Colleen Sabol Olitsky

CONNECT THOUGHT TO ACTION

We commonly hear people talk about living their dream life, but what does that mean, and how do you create it?

I just turned forty-nine years old in February, and I absolutely feel like I am only getting better and happier. The longer I walk through life, the more I appreciate choosing things that align with what brings me and my loved ones joy and the more I choose gratitude, forgiveness and abundance.

This didn't happen by accident. I have been reading about personal growth for twenty years and have really started to study and implement the concepts in the past thirteen of those twenty years. I have had amazing success as a result of applying fundamental principles, day in and day out.

The principles always work, all you need to do is learn them and put them to work for you. After studying personal growth and professional achievement, both at home and at work, for two decades, I know that there is a proven method to setting and achieving your goals. I am excited to share a few of them with you, along with my personal story.

Like all of you, I have been on a journey throughout my life, filled with ups and downs, but I do feel like I have always been willing to make a change when I wasn't happy, even when it wasn't the popular choice or if it was downright scary to do so.

The first step in elevating your life is both wanting to make a change and then understanding that you are responsible for your life, both the good and the bad. This can sometimes be a tough pill to swallow, but when we take accountability for our lives, it gives us hope that our future can be different. Even as a child and young adult, when things didn't go my way, I didn't play the victim; instead, I chose to "fight" and do something about it.

I chose to fight when I was twelve years old and was told I couldn't play on the boy's travel soccer team. Remember, this is almost forty years ago and there wasn't a girls team for me to play on.

I chose to fight after I got cut from my college field hockey team during my freshman year. I worked on my skills and mindset every day for a year until the tryouts the following fall, and I made it.

I chose to fight for myself after I had gotten lost in a downward spiral of partying during my first two years of college. My GPA wasn't strong enough to get into a medical or dental school; I even got mocked by my college advisor for even thinking I could apply. I chose to do something about it and got a 4.0 in my last two years and got into dental school.

I chose to fight when I found myself dating a guy who wasn't helping me be a better person.

I chose to fight when I didn't pass the Florida boards the 1st time I took them.

I chose to fight when we got a marketing violation from the State Board during our first year in practice.

I am using the word "fight," but not in a negative connotation. I also mean that I advocated for myself. I chose to take accountability for my life and take action to make the changes required to shift my energy and my life. This can be done in a productive and predictable way.

One of my biggest challenges was in my late thirties when I found myself unhappy with being a dentist. This was a profession that I had spent eight years and $250,000 to pursue. I loved it when I first got started, but as the years went by, I found myself doubting that dentistry was what I wanted to do for the rest of my life.

I was resenting my time at the office and missing the precious moments with my two young kids. I always felt I was in my husband's shadow as he began to soar with his cosmetic dentistry career. Instead of continuing down this path of feeling misery for years to come, I chose to fight.

I knew I needed a change, but what could I do where I could still help people and make an income? I thought about making a career change for almost two years before finally saying yes to something I had initially said no to, simply because I didn't know what I didn't know.

But thankfully, I got introduced to network marketing and fell in love with it. My desire to leave dentistry was so strong that it made me do whatever was necessary to build my new business; I was willing to talk to however many people I had to in order to begin earning enough with my side hustle so that I would be able to quit being a dentist.

After about fourteen months, I retired from dentistry and pursued my new career full-time. This did not go over well with just about everyone in my life. People thought I was crazy to quit being a dentist to go "sell shakes." But I knew deep in my soul that I needed to make a change for my own happiness, so I made it, and it turned out to be such a blessing.

For the next eight years, I lived my dream life. I had time and money freedom. I loved my job! It was a profession where I still got to help people in every aspect of their lives. I got to be a present mom for my two kids. I went to the gym every day. I learned how to play tennis a few years ago. I even wrote five books. I had it all!

"Success is the progressive realization of a worthy ideal."
- Earl Nightingale

I love growing myself and being challenged, so when I became complacent and not loving the changes being made at the corporate level of my company, I began to feel less great about myself or my future. A few other factors had me start doubting I could succeed at the level I wanted.

We think that if we have every comfort available to us, we'll be happy. We tend to equate comfort with happiness. But sometimes, we can become so comfortable that we are miserable. Comfort breeds boredom and low engagement with your life. It is overrated and often leads to discontent. Conversely, discomfort is a catalyst for change and growth. It forces us to adapt and stretch. Actively working to achieve our goals creates personal engagement, satisfaction, and overall happiness.

At the time when I had fallen into this comfort trap, I was earning $10-15K a month. It was passive income and it was incredible. I was grateful for it, but I had gotten so discouraged that it just didn't feel like a good fit anymore. I felt like a fraud. People weren't having the success that I wanted them to have. I was also starting to feel bored. I wanted more. I wanted to impact more people in a bigger way, and I wasn't sure this was going to be the right path for me to do so.

During this time, an opportunity came my way; I wasn't looking for it, but a message popped into my Facebook Account, and I saw a chance to join a new company on the ground floor. A chance to be partnered with some very successful people. A chance to be a part of the beginning and really have a voice in the company's growth and direction.

I took about twenty-four hours to research the CEO, products, and compensation plan, then decided to jump all in. It was not an easy decision. I was walking away from an organization of 13,000 people, a great residual income, and all of the relationships I had built over the past eight and a half years. It would all go to zero. I would have to start all over from scratch. But something in my gut told me to have faith and jump, so I did.

And wow!! It has been an incredible year. The right people showed up. I had amazing leaders who both loved me and pushed me so I could grow and serve at a higher level. I had my best year financially as well! All because I had the courage to ask what if?!?

"If you want something you have never had, you must be willing to do something you have never done." - Thomas Jefferson

To elevate yourself means that you're taking that extra step to do more than what is expected. It means that you have decided to start achieving those dreams that seem unrealistic. You have finally realized that you have the potential and the willpower to succeed, and now you want to put all those things into action. Getting to a place where you feel secure, stress-free, happy, and grateful can be a very rocky and difficult journey. It's a learning process where plenty of mistakes will be made and to be learned from. This kind of change can happen in a year or even as short as a month.

This type of transformation is absolutely possible. There are two main things that you'll need to get started: the right mindset and the ability to manage time efficiently so you can take the necessary actions. Although I can't promise you a full 180-degree spin on your life, I hope I can inspire and motivate you to start making some changes and start the process of elevating your life.

"If it is important to you, you will find a way. If not, you'll find an excuse." - Ryan Blair

Leaving a comfortable place to pursue something even greater is difficult. It's downright scary; trust me, I get it! But you cannot let fear control you or your life. Have the courage to fight for what you want. It was such a weird feeling to give up the very thing I had been clinging to so tightly to have this new path unfold. When I made my final decision to leave my prior company to start over with the new one, I knew I had to go all in.

Is there any other way? I made a decision. I committed. I told everyone that I was doing it again, but this time, I'd be going bigger, better, and faster, and I invited them to join me. Out of respect, I called my sponsor and let her know that I wouldn't be actively building my business anymore. I naively assumed I would continue to receive my commissions for the work I had done over the past eight and a half years.

The very next day, my account was terminated, and I lost everything I had built: the relationships and the income. I had a non-compete, so I couldn't bring my old team with me, and I was threatened with lawsuits if I did.

This absolutely fueled my fire! I was not going to play the victim. Once again, I chose to fight! I proceeded very carefully not to connect with existing teammates, which was a little sad for me because I knew they were missing this awesome opportunity. Yet I was also excited to get to start over, with a whole new team. New energy. New relationships. New opportunities.

I actually went back to all of the people who had told me no years prior, and guess what? This time, they were saying yes! They had watched my success over the years. They saw my heart, my habits, my relentlessness to serve my team, and my consistency, and they were excited to link arms this time and do it together. I started hosting pre-launch opportunity meetings at my house and helped new teammates present at their homes.

This thing literally started blowing up right before my eyes. I was reaching out to people about this ground-floor opportunity, and the people who used to run from me actually started joining me. People I had on my dream team list were saying yes, and it was taking off. I was working sixteen hours a day. My phone was constantly buzzing with calls and texts. I lost six pounds that first week because I was too busy to eat. It was crazy. But wow, was it oh so exhilarating?

Building something new. Creating what you always knew you could. Using your gift and talents in ways you had always wanted to. It was not easy. It was hard work for sure, but the rewards were worth it. I continued at a very fast pace for months. Most people are never willing to push themselves to see what they can truly become. It's ok to be obsessed when pursuing a goal. Balance may be out of whack during this period, and that's fine. Have a discussion with your family so they can understand and support you. It's not forever, just a sprint amongst the marathon.

But this was not about me, not this time. With my first company, I was working to create time and money freedom, and I had ultimately achieved that. But it was a selfish goal and I got bored. I knew this time; it was for others. It was to help show other people another way. To open them to a different vehicle that could bring some freedom into their lives. I did not do this alone. I did have my past experience, but I also had two mentors who both loved and pushed me.

They challenged me and helped me grow as a leader. When you have someone willing to help you, be open and be coachable. This is not the time for ego. If you are going to succeed, then you have to learn. Seek counsel from those who have gone first, they know what it takes. I used all of the habits I had developed over the years to make this new venture as successful as it was.

Back to happiness and success … so where are you in life right now? Would you say that you are winning? Are you happy? Healthy? Wealthy? In love? Or do you feel that you are in a losing season right now? Do you know you could be more, have more, do more? Would you be willing to sacrifice what's comfortable to achieve the extraordinary?

And success, what does it mean anyway? You have to consider success in all areas of your life and having your life designed exactly how you wish it to be, yet being open to the unknown and that God may have something even better in store for you. The whole happy, healthy, wealthy and in love…having it all.

"Success without fulfillment is the ultimate failure."
- Tony Robbins

Success means different things to different people. We know this, but self-love, inner peace, and fulfillment are foundational. It takes work to move into these spaces; it doesn't happen by accident. You have to make a decision, a choice, on how you show up and how you live this life. You have to be consistent and intentional with your mindset and actions to create what we consider a dream life.

Ideally, we want both achievement and fulfillment. Fulfillment is an art, not a science. There is no formula for what lights you up. Only you know what that truly is. We all have a different view of what we find fulfilling.

I've been there. I had "it all" at one point, and yet I was miserable, as I shared earlier. It happened twice over the last thirty years. Once in my late thirties when I knew dentistry wasn't my future, then again a decade later, when I had five times the net worth, I had the multi-million dollar home, I had the $150K car, we took $25K family vacations, we'd drop $500 on a meal and not blink twice, but I was frustrated because my work didn't align with who I was becoming.

I was grateful, yes, because I worked on being grateful, but at my core, I was lacking peace, and it felt awful. Something had to give. This hurt more than failure because I was okay with failing; it meant I was trying, I was growing, but to feel unfulfilled—ugh, that felt like the ultimate failure. Money certainly isn't everything.

But what does it take to make a change in your life? I will tell you this: it's not sexy nor is it always fun, but habits and self-discipline are absolutely critical! And knowing your why. Everyone wants to improve their life but they don't know how or what it takes. Or they know the how, but can't figure out why they won't do what it is they know they need to. We all know how to be healthier, we don't; need another book or podcast on what to do. It's the why, the why aren't you doing it, that needs to be examined.

I believe the problem stems from two different subjects, one being the idea of knowing what it is that you want and learning how to dream again in the 1st place. Moreover, number two is actually doing it, taking the necessary actions to make it happen. Everything we see in the physical world was created twice, once in the mind and then in reality. There are many experts on these two subjects and they are equally important, but how do we connect thought to action and truly start living our dream life?

Think and Grow Rich is one of the most famous books on self-development, but I would have tweaked the title ...

Think and Grow Strong, Act and Grow Rich. Connect thought to action. Books such as Napoleon Hill, The Secret, and The Law Of Attraction all focus on thought, which is important but it doesn't work alone.

Then we have people like Grant Cardone and Gary Vee. These thought leaders focus on action. Again, action is very important, but it doesn't work alone.

Can we marry these two concepts and connect thought to action? It is here, there lies a gap, and it's in this gap that people forget to dream; they let fear hold them back and allow their past to carry over into their futures. That gap resembles fears, doubts, and roadblocks, but it can also contain your inner drive, grit, purpose, passion, and why.

How do we learn that middle part and connect the two?

"Knowing is not enough, we must apply.
Willing is not enough, we must do."
- Bruce Lee

I have a very distinct moment when I discovered this little secret of connecting thought to action. As I mentioned, I began reading books in 2004 when a dental coach suggested a book list. I devoured Steven Covey's *7 Habits of Highly Effective People*. I continued racing through books for the next six to seven years. I'm sure some affected my actions, but never intentionally. Intention. Not until June 2011, when I was re-reading Jack Canfield's *The Success Principles*, did something click for me. Duh! You have to actually do something with what you're reading and learning. That's where my life really began to take off!

I enjoy reading about and teaching both mindset/goal setting and habits/taking action. I love those topics, but it's that middle part, that bridge between the two, that I feel stops most people from getting what they want. We must be willing to work on our own fears and doubts and build a stronger mindset to be prepared enough to take action. I think about this often, not only for myself but also for how I can help relay this information to others.

Here is a peek into my brain and how my mind thinks; A few years ago, I was lying in bed early one morning as I wrote down these thoughts. My son was sleeping beside me, all cuddled and nestled into my body. Our kids slept with us for like ten years. I absolutely loved feeling their bodies against mine.

So, at this moment, I had a choice. One voice urged me to get up and put these ideas on paper because it's it. (I have incredible thoughts/conversations in my head in the early morning and usually forget most of the wording by the time I get up, so I know I should listen to that voice.) But the other voice told me to stay in bed because it felt so good (warm, comfy, and loving).

Which voice is right? Grant Cardone and GaryVee would say get the F up and get to work. Deepak and Eckhart Tolle would suggest savoring the moment, being present, and being content. How does one balance those two contradictory voices? So, I compromised. I turned over and grabbed my phone to put my words "on paper" so I could capture these early morning thoughts while still being in bed with my son.

Balance. It's a tricky thing. To achieve massive success in an area of your life, you will have to sacrifice, and you will have to be thrown out of whack for a period of time. It is an odd dichotomy, for sure. When do we do what? How do we decide? I believe in seasons. Some seasons are filled with hard work and sacrifice, yet others are more relaxed where we enjoy what we have created.

Elevating your life requires unwavering commitment and a decisive mindset. It demands the self-discipline to choose actions that uplift your existence. To transform your life, you must realign your priorities and consistently alter your behaviors, thereby reshaping your habits and ultimately redefining your identity. How do you resist succumbing to the hardships that arise?

How do we confront challenges, glean lessons from them, and evolve? It boils down to choice. We always have the power to choose. With each hurdle conquered, we strengthen our resolve. Discover the art of advocating for the life you truly deserve. Don't allow overwhelm in your life; instead, master the art of pausing, taking action where you can, and relinquishing control, trusting in the unfolding of events. Breath, release, and let go is a phrase I commonly say to myself.

"The only way we can change our lives is to change our energy — to change the electromagnetic field we are constantly broadcasting. In other words, to change our state of being, we have to change how we think and how we feel."

- Joe Dispenza

We can't let our present reality, our current environment, dictate how we feel. If we can change the way we think and the way we feel we can produce the outcome we desire. We are the creators of our lives. Stop being the victim and begin to think greater than your current circumstances. Can you feel different in the presence of the circumstance and truly begin to create a different outcome? Learning means making new connections in your brain. The more you repeat a thought, choice, behavior, experience, or emotion, the more those neurons fire and wire together, and the more they will sustain a long-term relationship.

You have the ability to create your future reality; but you have to know what you want and then how to pursue it. Fundamentals, patterns, laws, and rules must be applied to the various areas of your life, e.g., health, money, love, happiness, community, charity, etc. Start reading books on personal development, and begin listening to motivational podcasts. Start creating success habits in your life, one day at a time until it becomes who you are. Moreover, as you elevate your energy and vibration, who and what you attract also begin to shift, and the things you've asked for begin to show up.

As you continue reading the beautiful chapters in this book, give yourself permission to start dreaming again and initiate taking the necessary actions to design your best life. Get a journal and begin taking notes and writing down what you want. What is your dream life? Picture how you want your life to be, get clear on what this looks like and write it out in detail. For real, pen to paper! Don't hold back or feel you're unworthy.

This is where self-development comes in. Begin listening to self-development podcasts and become more deliberate about what you think and feel. Reprogram yourself through repetition and emotion. Repeat these new thought patterns over and over until these new beliefs are automatic. Be raw, be honest, and be unapologetic. Focus on what it is you want more of in your life.

Believe that it is possible, and start moving in that direction, today! Begin creating the mindset, skills and habits to create success in your life. Know that it takes practice, discipline, hard work, and sacrifice. Stay the course, have persistence, and don't give up. This is YOUR life, and it's about time to create it the way you want it to be!

“Day by day elevate yourself to a breathtaking level by working on your passions.”

~ Hiral Nagda

CHAPTER THREE

Becoming an Angel

By Rebecca Shannon

I am Source's Pink Angel, but that is not who I was when this story begins…

I read a powerful book, *The Ultimate Coach*, written by Amy Hardison, which spoke to every part of my being. It is written about a man called Steve Hardison. When I read this book, I felt quiet, knowing my life was about to change. I knew I would meet and work with Steve.

Please forgive me as I am getting ahead of myself. Where does this story begin? It could be fifty years ago when I was born, or when, as a three-year-old, I started doubting who I was; it could be when I became a mum, broke my own heart, or got divorced. But this story, or at least this chapter, began on Christmas Day, 2021.

It was the end of a tough year. Having worked through the final stages of separation, we sold the family home and moved into a beautiful but temporary farmhouse. Our time there was a gift and a miracle. I have three boys; the two eldest are teenagers, and the years of separation have been hard for them, too. Much had changed in their world; there had been a significant shift in the family dynamic. In the post-COVID world, they lived half their lives with me and half with their dad. This was their first Christmas with just me, and our first in a new home.

A year into the pandemic, we were back in a winter lockdown in the UK, which meant we were on our own for the day. I was nervous about creating a Christmas for my children that would be special, that they would enjoy and that would distract them from all the changes they had seen that year. And as I did often then, I tried. I tried hard to create the perfect day, perhaps too hard.

The boys had woken up early, ripped all the wrapping from their presents, and were done opening everything before ten in the morning. We had a whole day stretching ahead of us. Some hours later, I sat alone at the table with the barely eaten Christmas dinner and all the trimmings. It had not gone well no matter how hard I had tried.

I retreated to my room and sat on my bed. Amongst some other things on my bedside cabinet was a thick black book with a large white exclamation mark on the front. I reached over and picked it up. I bought the book some weeks ago. As I sat there feeling sorry for myself, I looked at this book, and thought, "I don't know what else I can do now, so I'm going to read this book."

Rather than endorsements, there is an invitation from Steve on the back cover. I share these words, with the same invitation for you for this chapter and this story. Read this about you and create your own remarkable experience as I share mine.

"Please do not read this book about me. Read this book about you. Read it about being. And as you read, ask yourself, who would I need to be to be a more loving person? Who would I need to be to be a more effective parent? Who would I need to be to create a remarkable level of confidence? Who would I need to be to be at peace with who I am? Who would I need to be to be fully in love with myself and my life? Who would I need to be to live the most extraordinary life possible? I promise you that if you read this book with the intention of expanding your state of being, you will do exactly that. Your experience will be remarkable. Who you are being is everything."

I read that, and I read the first few pages. I read, and I read, and as I turned the pages, more and more words resonated with me. My subconscious accepted Steve's invitation; I was reading it about me. I was allowing my thinking to expand. Who I was being was changing. I read about Steve as a coach and how people experienced him and heard a voice in my head, saying, "Wow, I think that's who I am."

Then my little voice said, "No, this is Steve Hardison, he's The Ultimate Coach. Who are you to believe that you're anything like him?" This is a voice I am more familiar with. It doubts me; it may be little, but it is loud and overbearing. It doesn't want me to believe what I was reading could be about me. That voice would like to keep me small. But I kept reading, and something else became possible; I stayed with the intention Steve had invited me to. Who I was being began to shift.

Life carried on, Christmas was over, and a new year began. And who I was becoming made a crazy decision—I would go to Phoenix, meet Steve, and create this extraordinary experience. I would be the person who would invest in this life-changing gift for me. This was different; this was a seismic shift in thinking. This was stretching my comfort zone. I didn't do things like this; I wasn't an international jet setter with the time, money, or freedom to nip across the Atlantic for a meeting!

But I didn't let that stop me. I learned about creating the I am document from the book, a declaration of who I will be. The document creates a powerful shift from "This is just who I am" to *This is who I will be.* I was working on my document with my coaches at the time. In the coaching school I was in, I committed to create myself with my I Am document daily and put £10 into a savings pot each day for a 'Be With' session with Steve.

If you want to work with Steve, as I learned from the book, you go to him! A 'Be With' session with Steve costs $10,000. I declared I would be the person who went to Phoenix, Arizona. I would be one of the people who could share this experience in a future book! (Look how powerfully I created that!)

The truth is, the familiar voice in my head didn't quite believe this could happen. This was a huge sum of money and flying across the world to spend two hours with a coach, even the ultimate coach, seemed, at times, nothing short of ridiculous. And yet, this was the beginning of the experience I was creating and my work with Steve. A black hole was created by declaring my intention and making the commitment, and everything pulled towards it. Synchronicities and miracles started happening and the money I invested in my savings pot grew. And as it did, so too did my commitment. I created powerfully in my coaching practice and increased what I put away each day to £50.

As time passed, I showed up in my life, looking after my children, coaching my clients, and building my business. We had to move to a new house again, and the following months were possibly the hardest I've known. With a new awareness of who I was being, I was questioning more and more in my life, and I didn't always like the answers.

The voice that made me doubt I could ever be the person I wanted to be was getting louder. I kept showing up for everyone else, helping the people I coach, helping them to see beyond their judgments and beliefs, and yet I was struggling to do this for myself. My thinking was creating a lot of scarcity and separation in my life. The lack of a permanent home, fears about my relationships with my children, and fears about my new financial independence and responsibilities.

Instead of trying to shut it out, I listened. I heard how deeply I was hurting. I heard the fear. I listened as I felt how much I had lost. I heard how I needed to heal, forgive, and let go. I heard just how vulnerable that voice was, and that part of this journey was to let her be heard.

As I allowed myself to be with this vulnerable part of me, I realized I had saved all the money I needed to complete my declaration. The pot was full. I could go to Phoenix, Arizona! This extraordinary adventure could happen. The first thing I thought was, "Who am I to think I can do that? Who am I to go and spend that money?"

I was then at our cottage in Wales with my boys and friends. I went for a walk to think. In the local town, many shops had shut down due to the pandemic, in one of the empty shop windows, pinned up was a piece of paper. On it was an exclamation mark, hand drawn and exactly like the one on the book's cover. I didn't know why it was there, but what I did know was that this was my sign. I was going to Phoenix and would be with The Ultimate Coach.

I sent a message to Steve and read his reply. I wired the money. On the 29th of November 2022, my phone rang. It was Steve, and the nerves kicked in. "I can't speak to him; I can't take this call," I thought. And reality kicked in! "Hang on a second, you are planning to fly across the world to see him, so you better pick up the phone." We spoke, and he asked me when I wanted to come.

My conscious mind was keen to push it as far away into the future as I could, knowing that in the commitment I was making to be there, everything would be different, I would be different. And I guess I already was as I heard myself saying, "How would the end of January be for you?"

The call ended, and I had a date: 10:00 AM on 30 January 2023, in the office at his home in Mesa, Phoenix, Arizona, with Steve Hardison, The Ultimate Coach!

The rest of the year felt like the universe was making sure I would go and get what I went for! There was heartbreak, health problems, family issues, money challenges and more! And yet, a part of me was beginning to believe this would all be okay. The work had begun, and the black hole was pulling me in. The commitment was carrying me forward, and the end of January arrived before I knew it.

I was as nervous as I was excited, this was unlike anything I had ever done. I was going alone; it wasn't a holiday package, and no one was waiting for me at the other end. This was a whole new experience, a journey, a pilgrimage. I knew that something quite incredible would happen when I was there.

We had been in contact in the lead-up to my session. Steve had sent me things to read, and I had been sharing what I knew I wanted to talk to him about—breadcrumbs I needed him to follow. I needed that trail. I didn't want to go and not do the work I knew I needed. I was letting him know where I needed to go. I was already creating who I needed to be.

The day finally came, and I arrived safely in Arizona. Everything went perfectly. I stayed at the most wonderful hotel and met the most incredible people. Everybody on that journey was wonderful, warm and loving. I stayed for a week, and in addition to my time with Steve, I traveled to the Grand Canyon and created memories that will stay with me forever.

As for Steve Hardison, I could write forever about my time with him. Everything I'd read in the book is how it was. I was not disappointed. And why? Because that is how I had created it to be. That is who I was being. It wasn't just Steve who made me feel like I was the most important person in the world. When I arrived at his home in Mesa, the flag was flying for me. Everything was as I had created it, from reading the book about me.

It was like I was the leading character in my favorite film, which I watched repeatedly. We met on the porch, where I had been waiting. I was early. Steve welcomed me; he was dressed intentionally in pink for me. We chatted as Steve showed me around his beautiful home. His whole life, his home, and his family are a creation of the work that he has done over the last thirty years.

He showed me the gifts people had given him, the pictures, where they were in his home, why they were there, and all the extraordinary stories behind them. Steve was already creating powerfully for me. He showed me there was no separation in his life, what he does, who he is, and who he is being.

From here, we went out into the garden, and to the 1111 wall. I had read all about this, in the book and the diary of the artist Steve had commissioned to create this. Underneath the stunning series of art along the wall are all the 'I am' statements of Steve's clients and family.

One of the pieces is a Phoenix, rising from the flames, which was very much a theme of my journey. Not just as I was here in Phoenix, this was a rebirth for me. I could feel it in all the stories and the other 'I am' statements behind the paintings. We walked around the garden; in everything he shared, there was an intention, a meaning that he was carefully choosing to land with me. I was present at it all. Soaking up all of it. My name was on a pillar at the bottom of the garden, amongst others who had been here with Steve. There was mine in black paint. I was here.

We walked to his office; the office is where the magic happens. I felt it when Steve opened the door and invited me in. I feel the power, the energy, all the work that's gone on in there. I feel all the possibilities that have been created, and the lives that have been changed. I know from the stories in the book, the gifts from his clients. From the pictures on the walls, a sailboat on the window and the trainers cast in bronze. And now here I am. I sit on the sofa opposite Steve in 'the office.'

It is so hard to put into words being there and what happened in the following two hours. It felt like forever and was over too soon. I could have said that I had never felt such love or such a presence as I did in that room, which wouldn't quite be true. I have felt something like this before. With my dad, when he held my hand on his last night on this earth and in the chapel of rest when I sat with him after he passed away. Pure love, unconditional and unfamiliar.

Steve said, "Where do you want to start? What do you want to create here today?"

I replied, "I want to create something different for myself. I want to create a different story. I want to create a different me from the one I have, the one in my head, and what I feel in my heart. I want peace. I want to come home. I want to be me."

Steve listened and said, "You know what? I don't normally do this work in a 'Be With' session. It's normally done over a few weeks, but you're here, and you're ready, and we are going to go here." And we did. I kept eye contact with Steve. I wanted that connection. I created it that way. I was not letting myself off the hook or leaving without going as deep as I needed.

Steve asked me to write down all the things I believed about myself. He made me really go there, to that place in my head. All those things I say to myself. I wrote them all down, and they poured out of me. All the unkind and horrible things. I won't even begin to tell you the words that were on that page. I can't share them. I wouldn't write them about anybody else, and I was sitting there writing about myself.

There was no judgment from Steve. Only love, deep listening and compassion. We spent time with what I had written. Line by line he helped me create something else. Steve kept inviting me by asking, "What else is possible, and what else? And what could be truer? What could be the biggest version of that?" We took what I said and together created something different from it, we created who I am. We created from an intention of love and my commitment to be in the room. To do the work, to create a new version of myself. A truer version. A declaration of who I *be*.

We changed those beliefs I had about myself into something full of love. At that moment, I felt everything shift, and I didn't believe those statements I'd written down anymore. I believed in what I was creating instead. I dropped all those judgments I had about myself.

Steve told me, "I don't think you've ever really forgiven yourself. I don't think you've ever really forgiven your judgments on yourself. I don't think you've ever really loved yourself until now." And then in that moment, I did.

I sat with Steve's wife, Amy when we left the office. Amy is an angel; she is pure love. As she held my hand, Steve said, "Share with Amy what you came into the room with, those statements that you said, and then share with her what we've created today." I found it incredibly hard to speak the words on my original list. I thought this was because I was with Amy, with an angel, and then I realized that was true. I was and that angel was me. I am Source's Pink Angel and those things I wrote down were not who I am.

Amy said, "I don't know any God who would see you that way." I cried. I chose not to see myself that way either.

Before we left the office, Steve spoke about how we are projectors, we run the film or who we are, and we project it out into the world. We get to choose what film reel we project. We are not who we have become. We are who we choose to be.

Before I knew it, my time with Steve was over. I went back to my hotel room, and I slept for hours. I was exhausted, utterly exhausted. I had let go of beliefs I had held for years; just like the Phoenix, I had risen from the ashes to rise again. I woke and everything was different. I was different. Nothing would be the same again. I spent the following hours alone, there was a deep peace and a presence with myself, my new self. There was unconditional love.

I feel that peace now. Life happens. And it will never be the same. I am not the same. I have risen again, and again in this extraordinary life I get to live. Everything is elevated. I am elevated. Who I am will never be the same again. I have risen to where I am and become who I want to be, soaring high.

I am no different from you; we all have the power to do this ourselves. We are always creating our world from who we believe we are and who we are being. If we are scared and fearful, separated, and worried, then that's what we will create in our lives. If we elevate who we are, change those old beliefs, and replace them with love, compassion, hope, and possibility, that's what we will create in our world.

I see how much I have created in my mind on my film reel. The film shows how I was not enough and didn't believe in myself or forgive myself. That was my story. It isn't anymore. This is who I am. This is my declaration.

I am Source's Pink Angel. I am divinity. I am infinite. I am everything heavenly. I am the universe, and the universe is me. I am in love. I am the storm, a cyclone of love, and love is created from all I am. I am the Lioness by my side. I am unique. I am extraordinary. I am becoming more and more alive in every moment I live. I am perfectly imperfect and imperfectly perfect.

I am kind and compassionate. I am living in the power of possibility. I am practicing my conscious living intentions daily and transforming my life. I am worth all I desire. I am brave enough to always come back to hope and possibility. I am a strong and energetic force of change and transformation for others. I am in action with being as much as with doing. I am learning to slow down. I am willing to allow all my thoughts, emotions, and feelings. I am loving, curious and generous with all of myself. The light, the dark and the messy.

I am the wise woman my inner child needs when she is wild and free or seeking comfort and safety. I am the inner child when my wise woman needs fun, joy, and play. I am creating a flow of abundance and wealth that I share in the world. I am strong. I am vulnerable. I am all the worth I will ever be. I am without judgments of myself or others and forgive myself and others for any judgments we have. I am learning that acceptance brings renewed energy and vitality to my life experience.

I trust life. Life is kind. Life is for me. I meet love and life with playful inquiry and innocent curiosity to be with what is emerging within and around me. I love my fierce protector and know that there is no pain too great that my heart cannot meet. The more I enjoy my experience in the world, and as it manifests, the more my agency and potential grow. I create hot pink ripples in the world that sparkle and shine.

I am creating the life I love to live. I am becoming who I need to be. I am being me.

My declaration is long, and the perfectionist in me would have me cut it back. I am perfectly imperfect, so I let it be. I carried on writing and let it flow. This is a declaration of who I am, and it will be exactly as I created it to be.

Just as I committed to my journey to Phoenix, my time with Steve was extraordinary. I get to commit to this experience changing everything, and it has. I get to commit to elevating my life by creating who I am.

It's not a silver bullet. The film continues and I get to run the reel every day. I get to forgive myself every day when I am not all of who I am. I get to work through the questions, what else is possible, and what else and what if something else were true. It's powerful. It's life-changing. I get to be my declaration and create an extraordinary life every day for the next fifty years.

And so can you, if you have read this about yourself. You get to declare who you are going to be. You get to run your film reel and project that into the world. You get to create who you are. You get to create your life.

"Own your morning…
Elevate your life."

~ Robin S. Sharma

CHAPTER FOUR

The Missing Piece

By Idaliz Romero

As I read the title of this chapter, I could not help but remember why I first embarked on this journey of elevating my life and the process that led me to where I am now.

I thought, "At my age, what is the point?" (I am no spring chicken). My second thought was, "What difference would it make?"

From the moment I started, I felt the pull toward change. In the beginning, I did what everyone else on this journey was doing: I read self-help books, listened to podcasts, attended countless webinars (and still do), presentations, and Zoom calls, and signed up for a dozen different courses (I even completed a few).

Every day, as I did the work, I felt like an onion whose layers were being peeled away, revealing something I did not know before or did not want to see. Some things were "aha" moments, but too many were painful as I continued to learn and look inside myself.

I have always been resilient no matter what challenges came into my life. I had experienced many times when I could have given up, but I did not, something kept urging me to continue my growth journey. Did not know why; I just knew I had to keep moving forward. I was searching for a reason why I would start this uncomfortable journey at this point in my life.

One day, as I was writing in my journal, the "Why" became noticeably clear to me. My purpose for this journey was for my children, grandchildren, and future generations as much as it was for myself. I wanted to break the family cycles. Which cycles am I referring to? The cycles of fears, self-doubts, and disbeliefs.

Growing up in a family where change and growth were not prevalent, I always yearned for change. I always felt that there was more to life than the one life that I was living. The opportunity to focus more on my self-development journey started at a very difficult time in my life, when emotional pain showed up. I desire to leave a legacy of change, possibilities, hopes, and dreams bigger than my pain, and it needed to start with myself.

The moment I understood my "why," I became more focused on elevating my life, thoughts, and dreams. That is when a shift happened. My thoughts and beliefs started changing. I connected with people on the same journey and others who had already passed this point. Self-development became my main goal. This goal does not have an ending because I am still continuously learning and growing.

Reading has always been my go-to place for any questions I have. I read every book that I heard about or that someone recommended, and from each book, I received a different nugget of wisdom. I listened to the best motivators, such as Tony Robbins, Jack Canfield, Mel Robbins, and many others. I felt like a sponge absorbing and putting all the information into practice. It was an exciting time for me as I saw this time as a new beginning, a second chance to live the life I wanted.

When was the last time you felt excited about learning something new?

I realized how much I did not know and how much I had been missing. I wanted to create a learning environment for myself so that I could share it with my adult children as well but there was only one problem, they were not interested in my new way of thinking. I had no one to share my newfound excitement with.

That did not discourage me from continuing my self-development journey and I started to search for those that had the same enthusiasm as I did. I found a new place to share what I was learning and, in the process, connected with amazing people who understood my desire for growth.

As I worked on myself, things showed up in my life that I had hidden because they were too painful, and I had no desire to revisit them. But I knew that if I was going to change and grow, I needed to revisit these memories.

At first, the fear of pain kept me from continuing. I would go days without doing any work on myself just to avoid the pain, but the longer I put it off and the more I pushed against it, the stronger those painful memories became. At the time, I did not understand that change had to happen inside before it could be reflected on the outside.

Writing has always been part of my life. It gave me a space to write about my frustration with not continuing. I was angry at myself. I then had to learn that in order to overcome what I was going through, I had to start being vulnerable and sharing my feelings. It became therapy for me. I knew that if I was sharing my feelings, others may be feeling the same way, and this would allow them to be vulnerable.

Not only did I read, but I also joined businesses, not as much for the income that I could generate but for the connections and leaders that I could learn from. Some of them did not work out but the friendships I made are still part of my life. True friends from Germany, Australia, the UK, Canada, and so many other places across the globe. It has been incredible to share my journey with so many amazing people.

How long has it been since I started on this path? I am not sure, but I do know that as I felt myself becoming a new and better version of myself, I kept feeling as if something was still missing. I did not know what it was, so I focused on continuous learning.

I turned my attention to my health, and I knew that I needed to make some changes, maybe that was what was missing. Along with self-development, I read books about health and nutrition. Soon, my health started to improve as I changed my eating habits. I tried to find an exercise I enjoyed (not a big fan of exercise). I love walking, so I found a walking exercise that I liked. I was feeling better every day but the nagging feeling continued. Time passed and an event took place that changed my family and my life.

Have you ever had an event that shook you to your core that changed your perspective on life, your beliefs, and yourself?

For me, it was the loss of my twelve-year-old grandson, who I lovingly called "Grandma's Angel." His loss was the culmination of many for me and I fell into a deep sadness. I could not handle another loss, especially this one, so I gave in to my sadness, and for a while, I was not myself until one night something happened. That night, as I was falling asleep, I saw a small but bright light in my room. I thought it must be the kitchen light under the door, but I looked at my bedroom door and found it was not that. In that light, I saw my beautiful boy dressed in all white and wearing a beautiful smile. (Tears are building up in my eyes as I write this).

He called me "Grandma" and that meant so much to me since he was severely autistic and non-verbal. I was in awe not just by the word but by him. He did not say much but what he did say changed me. My grandson said one word, "Angels," and he was gone. I cried myself to sleep and thought it must have been a dream, but in my heart, I knew it was not because of this new peaceful feeling in my heart.

I understand if you think I am crazy. For a moment, I thought I was, too. It will become more apparent as I continue.

Days passed by, and I had no idea of what the message meant until one day, as I was attending an online event, they announced a speaker. I had never heard of him, and I was about to log out of the event since the speakers I was interested in hearing from were all done. The introduction for this speaker caught my attention. The emcee called him the "Angel Whisperer." I stopped what I was doing to see if I heard it right and I did. There was this young man whom I had never seen or heard before, and I felt I needed to hear his presentation.

He spoke with an accent; I was not sure what it was until he mentioned he was from Scotland. I sat there listening to him speak. I felt this pull to continue listening and felt as if I needed to hear his message. I must admit this was totally new to me, and I was not sure why I was so enthralled by what he was saying.

I continued to listen intently to every word he said. His knowledge and understanding of angels were remarkable. He spoke openly about them, and I felt peaceful just listening to him speak. I felt a connection with what he was saying. Suddenly, I clearly saw my vision of my grandson and the word "angels" he said to me. At that moment I knew I needed to listen to this young man.

I was engrossed in his presentation and did not move until it finished. I had to learn more about him and what he was teaching. I researched his life, his works, and his credentials. I found books that he authored, and I delved into each one. I listened to his presentations, followed him on social media, and joined his email list (I practically became a stalker). I focused on one of his books (which is still on my nightstand) have read it more than once. By now you may be wondering why I am sharing all of this with you. The answer will become clear soon.

While I was "stalking" this person, I was making my own connection with angels. I have been meditating for years but now I add an extra layer to my meditation. I was still determining if I was doing it right, but it did not matter.

I started building my connection with angels, and before you ask, I have not seen one yet. But I can tell you without any hesitation that I have felt them. The moment I began, I felt a shift. I cannot explain it, but I felt this peace around me, especially when I was in my bedroom. It has become my sanctuary from the world.

So, how does this all connect to elevating my life?

Remember when I mentioned I felt I was missing something in my self-development?

I finally understood what I was missing.

I had changed my thoughts, improved my health, and changed my beliefs but I had forgotten one very important piece. I had forgotten to add a spiritual connection to my self-development journey. My spiritual connection was very low or almost nonexistent. I knew now my grandson wanted me to see what I was missing in my journey.

As I continued to learn, meditate, and pray things started happening for me. I was certainly changing on the inside, but change was starting to show on the outside, too. This was the missing piece of the puzzle that I needed to find for myself, and I could not have done it without the help of my grandson. He has been gone for almost three years now and whenever I think of him there are tears of joy because I know we still have a bond that can never be broken.

So, how has this elevated my life?

The changes did not happen right away or in a big burst but in small changes through my connection to something bigger than myself. My meditations are at a deeper level. There is a sense of peace and of purpose.

Receiving insights about where I am going and what I will do has become my new norm. I have been writing journals since I can remember, and when I was invited to collaborate on a book, I knew that this was where I needed to be.

Since I opened my heart to the belief that there are angels who guide and protect us, I have experienced so many instances of inspiration. I know this may be hard for many to accept or believe, but my experiences have strengthened my belief.

Two recent experiences left my heart so full of gratitude that I cannot find the words to express it properly. We all have a dream or a goal that has been in our hearts, but we have not taken the steps to achieve it. Mine has always been to write my story because I have always felt I can help others learn forgiveness even in the most difficult situations.

One morning, as I was deep in meditation connecting with "my angel," I received a clear message. It showed me what the cover of my book would look like and the name of the person who would design it. You can imagine my reaction. I was filled with awe and so much gratitude. This is all new to me and I still have a small seed of doubt. I tried to explain it away, but I should have known better.

That same night as I fell asleep, I received another message. So, I can't draw. Drawing is not one of my talents, even if my life depended on it. But at that moment I felt the need to get a pen and paper and draw the design for the cover. I was half asleep, but I did it. I messaged my friend and sent her the picture I drew (I asked her to please not laugh at my drawing.)

Her response came, and she said that it was the exact design she felt she needed to draw. I was unable to get back to sleep after that. My head and heart were battling with each other. My head was working on finding an explanation for everything that transpired that day, and my heart was accepting and grateful for the most beautiful experiences.

My life has been elevated to a whole new level for the past three years.

- I have learned to love and accept myself with my perfect imperfections.
- I have opened my mind and heart to so many possibilities and beliefs.
- There has been a level of connection with the angels, the universe, and myself.
- My healing has allowed me to see life from a different perspective.
- I have realized that I have the power to change my life.

All the pieces had to fall into place for me to grow, helping me to be the person I needed to be. Having mental and spiritual knowledge gave me the framework for the road I was on.

Each of us has a different path in life. My goal here is not to convince you to believe in angels, the spiritual world, the universe, or anything else.

My goal is simply to share how my determination to elevate my life in more ways than one aligned with my purpose. Through the pain of loss, an incredible new world opened for me. There is a connection in everything that happens in my life. The fact I called my grandson "Grandma's Angel" from the moment I laid eyes on him and the moment I started connecting with angels showed me this was all part of a greater plan.

Every book I have read, speakers I have listened to, and webinars I have attended have prepared me to open my heart to a different life from the one I thought I was meant to live. My healing and growth are not finished, as I still have so much more to learn about myself and my purpose. I am filled with nothing but gratitude for the growth and blessings in my life.

I have had the opportunity to collaborate with John on one book and have been given the privilege to collaborate on another. None of these things would have been possible if I had not taken that first step towards learning who I am and taking the initiative to start working on myself and my personal growth. But more importantly, my openness to listen to my heart and not my head made it possible for me to elevate my spiritual life as well.

I do not know what will happen next (no one does) but I know that I am ready because I have created a life and environment conducive to learning and spirituality.

Sharing this was not easy for me but I know in my heart that someone reading this may be ready to take that first to a new life and a new and better version of themselves.

Here's to elevating your life!

Know that you are not alone on this journey, you can always call on help from friends, mentors, family, angels, and the universe. Maybe someday I will read your story and know you are on your way to a better life where you will be the creator of your life and not the spectator.

I hope that as you read this, it becomes apparent how elevating my life and finding the missing piece I was searching for are connected.

"Elevate. Each day,
live to elevate yourself,
each day elevate one person.
Make elevation your religion
and you shall reach infinity."

- Harbhajan Singh Yogi

CHAPTER FIVE

Our Map for Growth

By Alessandro Gavello

Imagine the feeling as you resonate with your life and see yourself making your best decisions yet energetically and enthusiastically.

How are you doing this, and how did you get there?

A Practical Experience

As you are moving your eyes from one word to another, listening to the meaning of your own thoughts, you notice how your imagination can show you so much more than what someone could expect, just as quickly as allowing you to wonder about different opportunities that can be available to you, sooner than later, because it's only in the now that we can make the difference in our life, as we keep changing all the time. And it is okay to change, it is okay to improve, it is okay to grow.

When we think in terms of success and failure, we may simply judge and disregard that whatever happened to us brought us here. The good thing about the past is it's over, the wonderful thing about the future is it's yet to come, and the amazing thing about the present is it's here, now.

How often do we allow ourselves to simply accept who we are when we can be more? We can learn to be better today than yesterday, as we aim ourselves towards a mark. We do so because we know our brains are not wired to give us results. Our brains work in directions, and when you know how to direct your brain, you know how to direct your life.

What do you want for yourself that is under your control?

How easily can you imagine yourself living life, wonderfully involved in enjoying every moment, as you scrumptiously taste the freedom of knowing how to change on purpose? You can tell that you have better memories than others, and as you learn to select them and use the ones that would serve you best, you can go back, now, to a moment when you had a very good time, when you enjoyed yourself deeply and freely. Think about how much fun you can enjoy as your heart pounds and you bathe yourself in a wonderful sense of joy! How much fun can we experience?

How much inspiration can we create, now, on purpose?

How many emotions can we create, that would allow us to feel how we want to?

Change happens all the time. Let's direct it. Let's do it on purpose!

Too often, we believe in this illusion that changing on purpose requires a lot of time.

It just requires practice. Practice requires intention, intention requires direction.

What do you want for yourself that is under your control?

We can learn very quickly. We learned how to walk, we learned how to talk, we learned how to breathe, and we learned how to relate with ourselves and with others.

We

Are

Learning

machines.

Let's keep learning on purpose as we develop better habits to use every day, direct ourselves towards what we really want, keep practicing feeling good for no reason at all, and make it one of the most important skills of all.

We were born with a brain and a body, and it seems we didn't get the manual to best use them, letting us figure this out mostly on our own.

As we all do the best that we can with the resources available to us at any given moment, we can realize how much it's not about having resources; it's about how resourceful we can be as we learn to live with purpose and direction. There are no unresourceful people, only unresourceful states. As we can only experience one mental and emotional state at a time, how important can it be to know how to choose which mental and emotional state to live in at any given time?

What do you want for yourself that is under your control?

By mastering the right skills and having the right mindset, we can use the best methods available to make our lives our masterpieces.

How soon do you want to start this?

This was one of the experiences I led my students through a few months back. We were having a great time learning how to help ourselves and others, and we knew the importance of working at a different level of consciousness to really affect change.

Einstein said, "Problems can never be solved by the way of thinking that first created them."

Hence, for something to change, we need to change something.

The Map for Change

At a certain point in our lives, we made the conscious/unconscious decision to determine how much we were worth, who we were, how much money we could make, and the standards we were going to establish for ourselves in our relationships with other people and with ourselves (love, friendship, health, wealth).

At a certain point, all this became our personal/professional map. Our conscious/unconscious reference point. Based on that, we decided what was important and what we needed to believe in to allow this map to work.

Many years ago, I would have dreaded the idea of change, even if it was happening regardless of my opinion. If you think about it, nowadays, this could have been considered "offensive" and "inappropriate" by some. How dare life make all these changes without consulting me first? I do not approve. And still, it looks like life just does not give much of a fudge about what people find offensive or not, and it's up to us to choose to find better ways to make it work. Because, when I live at the peak of my life, I am simply doing Personal Freedom.

Freedom is not a thing. In the same way as Love, Inspiration, Mental Attitude, Motivation, Communication, and so on. They are linguistic constructs of our interpretation of reality as we perceive it. They are shortcuts, and as far as we can remember, we can use them to our advantage.

It's when we forget and believe that they are an actual "thing" that we start directing our thoughts in a less useful direction as we build our expectations based on how we do the action of thinking. As Richard Bandler says, "Disappointment requires adequate planning." We cannot be disappointed unless we've built an idea of how things should be for us to have inspiration, motivation, communication, happiness, and love (just to cite a few examples). If only that event would have happened in that way, if only this person would talk to me differently, if I would have gotten that promotion, because it should have happened, as I say so, and so on, and so on…

How easily can you imagine a more productive way of thinking, where you allow yourself to create more useful beliefs, where you are in charge of your life and direct yourself towards pleasure and satisfaction? This requires being able to choose.

Choose to take responsibility for your life, and think better producing more useful feelings and emotions as you decide to get up in the morning, curiously, productively: "How can I be better today than yesterday?" "How much more resourceful can I be today than yesterday?" "How much pleasure can I stand?" When we focus on what really matters, we can direct ourselves towards it.

Mapping Your Direction

When was the last time you read something or listened to someone that changed your perception of life for the better?

I was very lucky, as I had many chances to keep learning. A long, long, time ago, I had one of these opportunities as I chatted with a rafting enthusiast. He reminded me of a Renaissance pirate, with his ponytail and sideburns. His eyes lit up as he talked about the thrill of navigating the rapids and the adventures he lived. Amidst all the excitement, he shared a few nuggets of wisdom that really stuck with me.

His words and his use of language had a very charming nuance, with some archaic terms mixed with an interesting use of syntax.

"In the midst of all that whitewater," he explained, "lies a lesson for life itself." We were walking in the city center of Torino, Italy but it felt like we were getting ready to ride the currents.

“Focus not on the looming rocks or the overhanging logs, for in doing so, you may inadvertently steer your vessel towards them, leading to chaos and turmoil.”

I could really see the rocks, the logs… I could smell the water!

“Lead your crew with a steady hand and a clear vision, guiding them towards the open channels and calm waters ahead. It's not just about avoiding obstacles, you see, but about navigating purposefully, harnessing the currents to propel you toward your destination. In the face of adversity, remain resolute, for it is in overcoming challenges that true strength is forged, and the bonds of camaraderie are strengthened. So, amidst the tumult of the river, remember to keep your eyes fixed on the horizon and what really matters, where the promise of adventure awaits. Because it is in the moments of confusion that you need to be the beacon of clarity, guiding your crew through the swirling chaos with unwavering determination."

I was enthralled by his gestures, his voice, and his eyes. He was born to be a gleeman!

"Embrace the challenge, for the rapids define the journey, shaping us into the adventurers we are meant to be. So, let the water rush around you, let the thrill of the ride ignite your spirit, and let the lessons learned on the river flow into every aspect of your life. For in the midst of all that wild water lies not just a lesson, but a revelation: aye, it does… Within every challenge lies the opportunity for growth, camaraderie, and the ultimate adventure of living life to its fullest."

His words had a rhythm, like the ebb and flow of the river itself. They sparked something inside me, urging me to embrace challenges head-on, armed with determination and a clear goal: "It's not just about avoiding obstacles, but about navigating with purpose…"

How often are we aiming our lives away from problems, challenges, and difficulties, when it is our perception of the event, our way to label the experience that changes the experience itself? How can we make the most of what experiences we are aware of, to learn, to evolve, to improve, to change?

We never stay the same. Do you want to get better or to get worse?

Map Your Masteries

How many experiences stuck with you? How many of those experiences did you manage to learn from?

It was nighttime. It was always nighttime when the black belts trained. No lights, and no wearing glasses either. Just you, your instincts, skills, body, mindset, and intuition.

The first official black belt lesson is one of those events you remember for a very long time. Unless you get knocked out, then… Well…

Everybody but us, the seven newly promoted to be allowed to wear black, knew what was coming. It's a good place to be if you know how not to worry and you can face things as they come. After very quick formalities, we, the seven (that's what we called ourselves), got placed at the end of the dojo. Our Master gave us a very simple speech about making sure we can fit in and the need to prove it. Something that has existed for as long as humans, tribes, and groups of people had the need to prove they can be part of that group, that they belong; they deserve to be there…

As he was talking, I was paying attention, as well, to the fact that all the other black belts were now covering the windows around us, and that's when I knew that whatever test we had to pass to wear the black kimono was nothing compared to what was expecting us… Whatever it was, it would be on a completely different level.

Fast-forward four years later… During this black belt night, we were going to train with a bow and arrow. You see, in many aspects, our Master had always prioritized practice, above theory.

You cannot really learn how to ride a bike unless you do it. You can study it, but that won't teach you how to balance it. Sure, you may want to know the theory but it's by practicing that you actually make it happen… In this case, our bow and arrow theory lesson had been quite simple: This is the bow; this is the arrow. You use the bow to get the pointy side of the arrow into the target. That's how you hold them safely; that's how you use them efficaciously. Aim properly, only point it when you are ready to shoot, and only towards the target you want to hit.

The targets were placed at only eight meters on the floor, side by side, within a one-meter distance between each other, leaning against wooden dummies that we generally used for shuriken practice. One meter behind the targets there was a wall. There was a one-meter gap between each target.

Why is the placement of the targets important? Because, as people were shooting, we were required to move behind the targets, without getting hit by the random arrow flying in between the gaps.

Fast-forward two more years… Our Master was explaining how much a fight can be decided in moments. "One punch, one headbutt, and one kick between your legs can be enough to disable any martial artist for a good moment. Your black belt will be worth nothing if you cannot think, breathe, or act. You need to go beyond what may limit everyone else, you need to learn and remember the future. That's when everything happens simultaneously and you are instinctively aware of it. Let's learn to block one punch. Of course, you have done it before, so, this won't be much of a challenge.

Grab the blindfolds…"

Map Your Mindset

"Life is not what it's supposed to be. It's what it is. How you cope with it makes the difference."
- Virginia Satir

You see, it's not just about what happens to us. The magic happens in what we do with it, acting according to our personal matrix and map.

For more than fifteen years I suffered from chronic pain. If you ask me, it's a very long time.

It started in my twenties after my hand got hit with a stick during a martial arts training session. Nothing special. I got hit a lot, but my injury didn't behave as usual this time. It didn't heal in two or three days. It got worse. Much worse! It got to the point where my hand, wrist, and forearm were in so much pain I could barely move them.

I had plenty of tests, and the results said that there was nothing major—just a mild bruise. After a couple of weeks, it got less painful and stayed like that for years. Some days, it was better; some days, it was worse. It was like playing the lottery, and the prize was to be able to use my arm with less pain than usual. And, on some level, it became what I expected it to be, as in my mind I remembered being in pain in the Past, I was living in pain in the Present, and, as a consequence, it was "easy" to feel like that situation was going to stay the same in the Future. It was "ouchibly" comfortable. It was not that it wasn't bad… It really sucked! I just "adapted." And "adaptation" is both a gift and a curse. Of course, "adaptation" does not exist; it's something that, again, WE do. The secret is, how are we doing it and using it?

Well…

I still managed to do my martial arts training… Painfully.

I still managed to perform as a circus artist… Carefully.

I still managed to live my life… Worriedly.

I was living this experience in my mind and my body 24/7, starting with my arm, and then my back. I did that for more than 15 years…

Until I realized how much this had enslaved me, and limited me.

Until I realized how much time I wasted in feeling like crap.

Until I stopped fighting against it.

This is what I needed to learn:

To
soften
and
let
go.

I started to change how I was doing whatever I was doing.

I changed my attitude, my beliefs, and my map. You see, the right attitude is NOT something you have or don't have. It's something that you do! Your attitude is about how you communicate with yourself and how this influences how you act towards the outside world.

"When you change the way you think, you change the way you feel, and this changes what you can do." - Richard Bandler

As I allowed myself to be more curious about better things and grateful for many others, I started to ask better questions, directing my brain toward more useful opportunities. What once was "chronic" pain "*simply*" became a sensation. No labels. No expectations. Different internal dialogue. Different perception. Different results. That sensation wanted to communicate something to me, and as soon as I paid attention differently, the way it communicated changed.

This is something that got me closer to wanting to know more about how we function, how we think, and how we feel, and eventually led me to study more Neuro-Linguistic Programming and Hypnosis. I found them to be some of the most effective ways to access and change our own internal dialogue on purpose and, as a consequence, our own maps and our perception of the world. Because that really mattered to me, I wanted to study it with the original co-inventor of this discipline, Dr. Richard Bandler, who is defined by many as the Leonardo of our times.

Later, I learned about Darryl Anka and the five laws of the structure of existence. I wanted to include them here in case they would help you find more of what you were looking for!

Here they are:

1. **We exist**.

2. **Everything is here and now**, (space and time are an illusion, they are a projection of our consciousness. Darryl Anka is suggesting that everything exists all at once; it is all accessible right here, and we just have to change our frequency to access that because that's how they are separated).

3. **The one is the all, and the all is the one** (he states that there is only one thing, and everything is made out of the one thing, even if it seems different).

4. **What you put out is what you get back** (I find this quite interesting. He points out how we are already giving off the vibration, as it is our natural core, to attract what we need. If those things aren't manifesting, it's quite possibly because we are stopping the vibration from bringing them to us with negative and fear-based beliefs. So, it's not necessarily an issue of learning to attract; it's about learning to stop blocking what you can naturally attract. What beliefs, thoughts, feelings, and actions would serve us best, then?).

5. **Everything Changes, except the laws**. (perspective, experience, perceptions, beliefs… They all change, constantly. Remember, we change, all the time).

It's not just about being surprised by being able to instinctively lift your arm in a timely manner as you neatly block that one punch blindfolded (how the heck happened!?). Or having "your intuition" telling you, "If I were you, I would wait before stepping any further," as a badly released arrow flies a few inches from my head, completely missing the official targets and, gratefully, my eye, because I listened to that "hunch/premonition," to that unconscious thought (I can still "hear" how casually that voice in my head sounded "If I were you…") Or letting go of control, as you learn many things and prove yourself worth it to be there, where you feel you belong (and it's ok not to be perfect; keep learning and improving).

Because it's not just about what Rudyard Kipling wrote in his poem "If":

"[…]
If you can dream—and not make dreams your master;
    If you can think—and not make thoughts your aim;
If you can meet with Triumph and Disaster;
    And treat those two impostors just the same;
[…]

"If you can talk with crowds and keep your virtue,
    Or walk with Kings—nor lose the common touch,
If neither foes nor loving friends can hurt you,
    If all men count with you, but none too much;
If you can fill the unforgiving minute,
    With sixty seconds' worth of distance run,
Yours is the Earth and everything that's in it,
    And—which is more—you'll be a Man, my son!"

It is much more than that, and less… It is about the meaning and the learning and the gratitude you can do in regard to those experiences that are there to simply show you one thing, and more:

We are much more than we think we are. We can do much more once we realize that if we aim ourselves at what really matters, we can access different kinds of resources.

What matters to you, now?

And so, animated by the tales of that Renaissance pirate, I set out on my own adventures, I traveled the world, changed countries, changed jobs, lived, loved, laughed, cried, tackled whatever obstacles came my way, crashed into a few walls, changed course, fell, made errors, failed many times, and learned a few more things. I now know that within every rapid lie, the chance to discover my own strength, and in every twist, my own potential to repeatedly emerge anew.

When you can produce the right feelings, as you resonate to your tune and vibration, you can create a movie in the space of your mind long enough to allow you to realize your personal potential and give you direction toward the outcome you are looking for.

When you see yourself growing through the challenges as you get closer and closer to your goals because we all know that we do not have results, we have methods, we have habits, and based on those, our results will come, as you become what you repeatedly practice. What mindset do you have, what mastery are you acquiring, and what methods are you using to direct yourself toward your personal masterpiece?

When I live at the peak of my life, I do one important thing: Personal Freedom. And Freedom is something that you DO. In the same way as you do the action of communicating (more or less effectively), in the same way as you can motivate yourself, based on how you act and live your life (more or less productively).

In the same way, as you act during the day, lovingly. You can talk to someone, lovingly. You can relate with someone/yourself lovingly. And suddenly, you just created your experience of love, and because you start feeling good about yourself, more people will start to feel good in your company. It's just one of those things.

What tone of voice inspires, motivates, and makes you feel good? Make sure you use it when you want to feel that way in the right context. Attach great, powerful feelings to every activity you know is useful for your well-being.

Whatever tone of voice you use to demotivate you and make you feel bad… Learn to change it! Anytime you notice you are doing it, make it different. Change the tone of the voice; how would it sound like if Micky Mouse were saying it, or Donald Duck, or Goofy… Change the speed; make it very fast or slow as the pitch goes higher or lower. And as soon as you can make these choices, the feelings will modify as well. When you alter the way, you talk to yourself, you will alter the quality of the feelings you produce!

Life can be simple when you learn how to make it so.

Your life is yours to be lived and experienced. As you keep doing it, as much as you can, in your own personal way, and as you make it your own personal Masterpiece, you can wonder how you can live it more enjoyably today than yesterday and how much value you can add to the people around you, as you decide more useful beliefs enthusiastically, now!

Know yourself, others, and the world around you.

Make your life work for you, as you go, do, and lead by example.

“Only passions, great passions can elevate the soul to great things.”

~ Denis Diderot

CHAPTER SIX

Elevate Your Life: Reimagining The Nexus of Art

By Lynn Hayward

Section 1: Artistic Essence and CRPS Onset

In the realm where color meets canvas, my life as an artist flourished, embodying over forty years of creativity; art was my soul's truest expression. From the intricate designs of my youth as a textile designer to the alignment of colors and textures in my portfolio, I breathed life into whispers of extending my imagination.

Yet, a blatant shadow fell across this vibrancy with the onset of Complex Regional Pain Syndrome (CRPS). This unwelcome doppelgänger, similar to harsh red graffiti across a pristine masterpiece, threatened to obscure my identity and the very heart of my existence, challenging both the value and functionality of my being, my hands and upper limbs and the form of my creative expression. The air that I breathed.

In this transformation, my story deepened, symbolizing personal struggle and universal resilience. I would like you to stand alongside, to journey with me as we navigate this change and discover how an unexpected twist of fate can catalyze new forms of expression, healing, and hope.

In the crucible of my chronic pain, digital art emerged not merely as an aesthetic pursuit but as my sanctuary—a powerful quality for healing. The transition to digital mediums became a revelation, but it soon unfolded into a vast landscape of therapeutic exploration. Each digital stroke brought solace, silently combatting CRPS's pain. Creativity became my therapy—a silent rebellion against my symptoms. Art therapy offered a voice to my pain, ensuring it was heard and understood. In the alchemy of pixels and digital palettes, the bitterness of pain transformed into the balm of creation.

Section 2: Struggle and Adaptation

Initially, this pain was abstract—indescribable, elusive, and relentless. It washed away my freedoms and challenged me to find new ways to hold the brush and narrate my story. The transformation had begun, and while the future seemed obscured by a heavy fog of uncertainty, I unknowingly flickered the unwavering flame of a creator's sleeping spirit, dreaming to rewind. I had no mindset to adapt.

Twenty–four/seven, CRPS established a twisting, vice-gripping burning pressure with an intense hammering of pain that disrupted this harmony. My hands and upper limbs, once dexterous and certain, became instruments of torment. Formerly familiar friends, the tools of my craft turned into sources of frustration, as pain rewired my relationship with my soul, my art and my individual circumstances.

Bawling out the spasming shooting attacks; the realization of living, let alone the undertaking of creation, now became a battleground where each personal, emotional and artistic victory was hard-won against the relentless foe of pain. I could do very little for myself. Utterly useless in my negative spaces. I could see no way out. Imprisoned in a mindless, choiceless body, perpetually feeling under the microscope; ignored and dismissed. I was swiftly retired through illness at fifty-five years old! I felt, "put out to pasture in Antarctica."

Deprived of an income, nor any simple means to venture outside my walls easily. My life was spiraling out of control like a vertigo washing machine. A near total loss of independence. This was not me!

My journey with art as rehabilitation (willingly, alongside my other treatments) sluggishly wove a new thread into the fabric of my life's work. It became a testament to the resilience inherent within me and a beacon for others navigating the murky waters of chronic pain illness, including nerve pain.

My story unfolds in chiaroscuro, the stark contrast of light and shadow mirroring the sudden plunge from a life of tactile artistry into one where pain became my constant companion. The arrival of CRPS was the dark tonal background against which my life would now be contrasted, the defining moment where 'before' turned to 'after.'

Section 3: Transition and Evolution

In the 'before,' I reveled in the physical joys of art—the visceral spread of oils beneath a palette knife, the yielding surface welcoming bold strokes, the graceful dance of pencil on paper. My creations were born of the harmonious dialogue between my imagination and the physical world. I was attuned to the delicate interplay of texture and hue, pattern and light, and each swipe of color weaving was a visual symphony.

The digital world has become my haven for creation and transformation, allowing me to craft visual narratives that surpass my physical boundaries. Therefore, art bridges my inner world with others, connecting CRPS and other individuals with a broader community. Each creation elevates past adversity, encouraging reflection and gratitude.

In #asymphonyofechoes, I encapsulate my CRPS journey and its collective resonance, inviting others into a compassionate movement that validates every experience of pain.

My art, now infused with intentional mindfulness, showcases a palette of experiences. I invite onlookers to delve into the rich layers of my growth and vision, interpreting each textured piece in their own light.

Survival meant adapting, leading me to digital art—a necessary metamorphosis from tangible mediums. On the digital canvas, I found a world where creativity knew no physical bounds, where my artistic spirit could roam free from the shackles of CRPS. Voice-activated software and touch-sensitive screens became my new tools, allowing me to pour my vision into art without the tribulation of touch. This wasn't merely a change in medium, but a personal transformation.

I often tag with #thereisalwaysmethodinmymadness, I frequently explore beyond conventional boundaries, seeking the crystalline insights found in altered viewpoints. This explorative method is most strikingly manifested when I invert my canvas—a gesture that might seem to welcome chaos but, in fact, introduces a fresh coherence. This topsy-turvy perspective encourages me to approach my life and art at their primary cores, with every tint and shade liberated from their accustomed context.

This reversal transcends the mere act of physically reorienting the canvas; it signifies a thoughtful subversion of perspective, prompting my mind to detach from established ideas and grapple with art in its most unembellished form. In this inverted space, I engage more intimately with my creations, unobscured by habit or expectation, prompting a cerebral waltz of innovation and reassessment.

Like the upturned canvas that nurtures problem-solving and fresh examination, it mirrors the versatility I aim to achieve across all areas of life. This practice complements flexibility and patience, a readiness to appreciate the indefinite and unearth the harmony between method and what might be perceived as madness. The revelation it brings to the fore is transformative, offering a surface that echoes the potent ability to perceive the world—and my art—not only for what it is but for what it could be when viewed through a prism of endless potential.

Section 4: My themes, advocacy, and community narratives

My art evolved, intertwining my pain into a narrative of resilience and rediscovery. In this reimagined landscape of creativity, I found a new way to connect with myself and an audience, sharing not just my art but the essence of my journey. The emerging themes—pain and perseverance, vulnerability, and victory—mirror life with

CRPS, always highlights my reality. #DigiArt became my voice when words failed with foggy brain symptoms, my refuge and distraction when pain stormed the gates, and my medium to connect with a world that could not see my agony but could hopefully feel it through the colors and shapes that flowed from my right middle finger to my perceived digital brush.

My art, reflective of my CRPS journey, extends into a series of innovative coloring books. These are currently being designed to challenge serious colorists, offering intricate designs up to a "10/10" difficulty, while also providing simpler designs for those just dabbling. Beyond mere entertainment, they're a call to introspection and connection for my tribe.

My artistic endeavors are not just an act of creation but a profound exercise in self-advocacy and independent advocacy. The colors and textures I choose, the forms that emerge on the digital canvas—each is a deliberate expression designed to bring visibility to the complexities of CRPS. This art goes beyond aesthetics, as it seeks to educate, evoke empathy, and challenge the misconceptions surrounding chronic pain and disability.

I aspire to use my creativity for broader change, making digital art an inspiration for those with physical limitations, and driving tangible improvements for those with CRPS in particular. The digital realm, rich with connection and accessibility, awaits my full exploration. I'm building a website to foster shared experiences and artistic discovery. I continue to use platforms like YouTube, Facebook, Instagram, and TikTok to share the realities of CRPS and the healing power of art with bigger audiences.

Expanding my palette of creativity and activism, my desires extend beyond the canvas of digital art into the vast field of support and empathy.

With hashtags like #useyourvoiceempowermentechoes,#amplifyadvocacyforhealing and #fosteringsharedequalityletsmindfullyworktogether, I join hands with fellow warriors to amplify our voices for the rights and recognition of individuals with #chronicpainillnesses and #CRPS.

Through my art, I have found my people. This journey of mine—while deeply vulnerable and personal—resonates with a host of other stories, each varied in tone but unified in its essence. Engaging with others transcends mere storytelling; it is a harmonious mosaic. Social media platforms become stages where our collective narratives play out, creating a montage rich with shared pain, triumphs, and the everyday heroism of living with CRPS.

Each hashtag, from #highlightingdisabilitychronicpainhealthmatters to #CRPSawareness, is a rallying cry, a call to action. These are more than mere tags; they are the digital echoes of a movement, reaching out into the vastness of the online world to touch stranger's lives, unite voices, and amplify the message of resilience and recognition. I see your strength and spirit.

My advocacy weaves into society's fabric, adding vibrant hues of awareness. Alone, I'm one voice, but together, we form a persona for change. My skill is also my protest, solace, and a bridge to knowledge and understanding. It is an offer to look outside the surface, to see the world through the lens of compassion, and to recognize the power of our collective voices in creating ripples that turn into effects.

My heightening development matured past the picture, infiltrating, and lifting every aspect of my existence. It was in these reassessed values that some relationships deepened or were redefined. Community and support networks became integral to my survival. The connection with fellow artists and extraordinary individuals with CRPS provided a harmony of shared stories and strength, reinforcing the knowledge that while my path is unique, I do not walk it alone.

I am familiar with independent advocacy, having worked as a part-time Finance and Administration Manager and a Mental Health Advocate for an advocacy charity in Scotland. Therefore, advocacy efforts through visual language are virtually second nature for me. Creating textured patterns of vibrating language is a powerful strategy for engaging my audience.

The use of diverse mediums and digital platforms to reiterate and share my journey embodies the essence and patterning of these powerful hashtags embraced; aiming to resonate deeply with viewers and contribute to greater awareness and understanding of CRPS and its impacts. On X (Twitter) every November, I participate in a month-long campaign of:

- #NERVEmber
- #NervePain
- #CRPS
- #RSD
- #colortheworldorange
- #AlgoNeuroDystrophy
- #GoOrange
- #burning4aCURE

- #PAINttheworldorange
- #CRPSAwarenessMonth
- #NERVEpainawareness
- #NERVErgiveup

With @iPainOfficial, @BarbyIngle, @BNightsCRPS, @pain_europe, and @powerofpain, to name just a few pain warriors, I love taking part, including being one of the top contributors, sharing, and paying it forward.

Section 5: Resilience, Growth, and Ongoing Journey

My self-development, navigating the two-faced landscape of CRPS, has transcended an ordinary conflict with an unyielding adversary. It has unfolded into a kaleidoscope of personal transformation, each tesserae revolution imbuing the color vibrancy, rich in resilience and ever-renewing. Life with CRPS taught me the profound lessons of empathy, patience, and strength.

These are not abstract virtues but tangible necessities that became the virtual easel for traversing the daily merciless intricacies of the syndrome. The heightened sense of empathy allowed me to connect with other's pain, bridging the gap between isolated suffering and communal understanding. Patience became the rhythm of my days, teaching me to embrace the ebb and flow of my lesser physical capabilities.

Strength and adaptability converted my steadfast allies, not merely in confronting CRPS but also in reclaiming my identity as an artist and advocate. The resilience within me ignited a creative blueprint into the precise world of vector art. In this realm of digital drafts, each line and curve is a deliberate act, offering exactness and control that mirrors my own capacity for renovation.

My spirit, undeterred by physical constraints, found kinship with the vector's deliberate paths—each node and vector a conscious choice, akin to a draftsman's pen on a designer's plan. In vector art's potential for endless refinement and precision, I discovered a metaphor for my own inner strength: endlessly scalable, meticulously crafted, and enduringly expressive.

Forward-looking, my CRPS journey informs my aspirations and influences wider societal impacts. My guidance for those with CRPS draws from profound understanding and experience, carving a unique path that I've navigated, now extended to others. The odyssey unraveled has been rich with discovery, where each digital brushstroke and community engagement bears the imprint of elevation—a mantra that transcends personal affirmation and touches the realm of the multidimensional.

This artistic expansion into the fourth and fifth dimensions reaches beyond the present, harnessing time's narrative and the tapestry of possible realities to enrich my creative and advocacy efforts. It's an empowerment that envisions and constructs a boundless realm of creativity and growth.

Moving forward, I strive to position markers as signposts for others through guidance, distilled from my route of endurance. Promoting a mindful approach to life and creativity. I encourage embracing the concepts of the following tags:

- #aspiringriseabove — To reach past what we perceive as our limits.

- #standtallenduring — To remain steadfast amidst life's trials.
- #digdeepersearching — To uncover deeper truths and understanding.
- #abiggerpictureisrevealing — To acknowledge the vastness of our potential.
- #healfromwithininspiring — To nurture our inner well-being and inspire growth.

Therefore, I champion the pursuit of confronting personal barriers to soar to new creative heights. Mockery and doubt are adversaries of progress; instead, let us step forward with open hearts and minds, ensuring that our personal convictions and values are not diminished by our own controls. May we permit ourselves from the shackles of self-imposed limitations and rise on the wings of our newfound freedom and vision.

Section 6: My invitation and aspirations – elevate through art and my main purpose 360Forward

I extend encouragement to you: in the context of regeneration. Let us continue to heighten our existence, to streak our narratives with the indelible ink of resilience, empathy, and creativity. Together, let's craft our unique self-mastery that surpasses the constraints of CRPS or other barriers, interlacing the strands of our mutual capabilities into a collage of shared dreams and desires. Our journey of elevation and hope is ongoing, engaging your voice and substance. Together, with #WeElevate, #WeTransform, and #WeHope, we journey as artists on life's backdrop, each stroke affirming our ambition to soar past restrictions.

Connect with me in scaling beyond the visible horizon, to an abode where regrets fade and positive assertions of 'I CAN,' 'I AM,' and 'I HAVE' mark our ascent. In this shared space, we are the architects of purpose and destiny, capable of a make-over, an existence where the gravity of pain cannot constrain the optimism of our creative souls. Let us mark our route not by the weight of our challenges but by the lightness of our triumphs and the expansiveness of our dreams.

Together, let us redefine our ascent, not as a solitary surge but as a collective swell—building a tsunami of attitudes cresting in flow, towards a global freedom where pain is reimagined and recreated, where resourcefulness reigns supreme, and where courage is not just a fleeting dream but the very essence of our authenticity.

Elevating my life through creative expression is ultimately a statement about how I aim to boost my life and the lives of others. I suggest a commitment to exploring and sharing the richness, #ajourneyofrichesofhumanexperience, using art and words to transcend the borders of chronic pain and illuminate the path toward healing and empowerment.

Rooted in my personal ethos of 360-Degrees-Forward, I champion the fluidity of expression and the cageless potential within us all. By embracing the unconventional and nurturing a belief that sharing and caring forge powerful narratives, I journey through the pages of chapters and art to fuel personal growth. My commitment is resolute: to design a space where stories unfurl like brushstrokes on canvas, each motion an exploration of discovery, and the voyage from #pain2paint2purpose resonates with the richness of infinite abundance.

"No matter which way I AM facing
in my 360° space,
I AM always
'facing FORWARD' or
'FORWARD facing'.
Solutions I seek,
are consistently within reach.
It's awareness;
my intrinsic mindfulness
and redesigning choices,
that determine the quality
of my unique
'pay-it-forward' journey.
Surprises emerge
from my
'cocooned' perspectives."

This poem is my 360-degree forward definition as I stand in the present and reflect on my transformation into a digital artist (a domain that I vowed a long time ago never to enter) and how each moment of adversity has molded my observation, leading to intimate and artistic evolution. The idea of elevating life—#360DegreeForward—embodies my commitment to continuous growth, embracing each challenge as an opportunity to learn and expand.

Observing the world from a spherical perspective and beyond, with hashtags as signposts, the DNA of my digital advocacy, and weaving a broader narrative. They are my call to arms, my inspiration, and my triumph. These hashtags reflect where I've been, markers guiding me and my tribe toward a future where CRPS and other chronic illnesses are understood, art transcends pain, and every person's journey is valued and validated.

This journey is a testament to the power of naming our experiences, claiming our narratives, and connecting in a fragmented world. These beacons of hash-symbolled thoughts illuminate my path forward, each a step toward a brighter, more inclusive future.

I choose my hashtags deliberately, weaving them into the nuance of my advocacy and artistic expression. They're not just a part of my narrative; they're the pillars of it, offering structure and making my voice resonate across the digital landscape. I believe every day is a #ChooseDay to create the day your way.

With #pain2painT and #CRPSawareness, I'm not only chronicling my journey but also sculpting a virtual gallery where each of us, united by our struggles and victories, can rise together. My mission is to spark a movement that spreads far and wide, turning individual stories into a symphony of shared experience.

It's in the spirit of unity that I use hashtags like #sympathyvsempathy and #listenwithunderstanding, because I believe in the strength we garner when we stand together. Elevating our lives is more than a personal quest; it's about elevating one another to places we never imagined possible. My hashtags:

- #pain2painT
- #pain2painT2painLESS
- #pain2painT2painLESS2painTMORE

These tags highlight the arc of my creative exploration through art, art therapy, #writingfromtheheART, and poetry, blending my personal insights with the expansive possibilities of digital and AI collaboration. At the end of this chapter, I've included a selection of these poems; they all chart the evolution of my relationship with strife, pain, awareness, redesign, and elevation through my artistic process. Designing these poems is enjoyable, transporting an added dimension to my digital creativity. Distraction serves as another pain management strategy and a coping mechanism for me. Here's how I perceive and integrate these special hashtags into my narrative:

- **#pain2painT**: This hashtag marks the beginning of my conscious path, where I began reinterpreting and redesigning the physical and emotional pain of CRPS into my art, giving form to what was once abstract sensations. It's the alchemy of morphing pain into "virtual paint", confronting the agony while channeling it into creative energy. #FacingMyFear.
- **#pain2painT2painLESS**: Diving deeper into #creatingmydaymyway and imaginatively fostering a creative alliance with my CRPS, in the hope of #turningdownmypainvolume, I found that reimagining and recreating my debilitating pain symptoms, provided a form of respite, a distraction, or momentary relief from searing chronic pain. Unexpectedly, the process of therapy through digital painting did more than just visualize pain; it began to mitigate its impact on my consciousness, transitioning my experience from one of persistent suffering to a state where the pain was less overpowering and all-consuming.
- **#pain2painT2painLESS2painTMORE**: This hashtag signifies a further development in my journey. It's not just

> that art ‘reduces’ my pain; engaging with creativity brings about a profound joy that is its own form of ‘paint’—a positive and enriching experience that adds more to my life than CRPS can take away. It represents the transformative power of art to not only alleviate pain but augment my existence with a greater sense of fulfillment and purpose.

#MyHashtagsofElevation, like #BreakingMyMould and #BreakMyMouldTakingFlight, capture my journey of transcending CRPS limitations and societal norms. They reflect my pursuit of transforming obstacles into avenues for artistic growth. These hashtags are my rallying cry for turning pain into expression and affirming our control over our stories, emphasizing the power of collective support.

In integrating these hashtags into this chapter, I print a vibrant hashtag design of my digital advocacy, creative resilience, and a visionary outlook. If some specific hashtags or themes need further emphasis or a deeper exploration, I will incorporate those into my evolving narrative if appropriate. If I want to be included, I need to take part wholeheartedly. I am never too old for my journey to begin again, to be redesigned and reshaped. It is always my choice.

My awareness and use of hash symbols was born in 2021, a few days before I turned fifty five, unlocking that link of digital connection. Simple yet potent, these symbols became a pivotal part of #myarttherapy, helping to “optically mix” many advocacy and creative voice layers onto the vast infinite canvas of social media.

With hashtags like #pain2painT and #CRPSawareness, my posts transform into open invitations to a shared journey. They are not mere labels but the heartbeat of my drive, drawing in those who resonate with my experience of transforming pain into creative power.

The careful curation of these tags ensures they are the underpainting of my digital narrative. They sketch and reinforce my message, magnifying it within the digital expanse. Each tag, from #writingfromtheheART to #pain2painT2painLESS, dashes my story with continuous lost-and-found lines, graffitiing my struggle with pain and healing into a collective composition.

Aware of the pitfalls—clutter, irrelevance, misuse—I deliberately stumble the digital space. #Markmaking my way, I strive for a balance that turns hashtag narratives into motivations for real conversations, mindful of their reach and impact.

Through my chosen hashtags, I feather the collective colors of our shared struggles, forming bonds of memory and reflection that might otherwise remain hidden. They are not just a call to imperfect action but an emblem of bonding, an invitation to transcend individual challenges and trace an arc of geometric elevation.

In my considerations, these symbols stand as glinting threads, binding the various facets of my story—from strife to serenity, from solitary pain to shared understanding. They call upon the community to join in the storytelling of experiences, each line resonating with its own truth. These individual tags are the outpouring of my mixed media textures and emotions. Therefore, incorporating these fibres is not just an act of conclusion but an opening to an evolving dialogue. They affirm my dedication to creating my day my way, continually reshaping, and reimagining my journey of #CreatingTexturedPatternsOfVibratingLanguages, engaging deeply with the lived reality of CRPS.

My passage is an echo of humanity's collective resilience. Hashtags like #Iamanexpertofmeandmyexperiencesonly, #NERVErtheless #Istandalongside, serve as vignettes within our shared human experience—individual narratives painted into a grand fresco of strength and hope for all to partake.

Section 7: Conclusion and Atmospheric Perspective

Here's how my artistry embodies the core themes of #myjourney, not just as therapy or advocacy, but as a rich language depicting the intricate narrative of my life with CRPS. My art mirrors the complexity of what's often termed the 'suicide disease,' weaving a rich tapestry of emotions and details that reflect the strength I've developed. This depth is not confined to the observable three dimensions; it extends into the temporal flows and potential realities of the fourth and fifth dimensions, where time bends and multiple possibilities coexist, enriching my creative landscape.

As I etch my persistence and hope upon the digital canvas, I fervently amplify our collective narrative. By pushing the boundaries with #turningthepainthresholdup, we are shaping a world enriched with empathy and understanding #NOW. In this realm, our patterns forge new pinnacles, and the seascaped skies respond with the commanding force of a thunderstorm's atmospheric perspective, a metaphor for the tumultuous yet transformative nature of my artistic exploration.

We are drawn towards milestones of growth and connection. Here, allow your imagination the courage to explore new perspectives on your personal transformation and journey. Using #mindfulnesschoices and #creativitybeckonsus, place yourself within Figure 1: 'Elevate Your New Beginning,' which embodies my #360DegreeForward philosophy. This illustration serves as my gateway into the fourth dimension, where time is not my barrier but a canvas, and the fifth dimension, where each choice creates my new reality—how do you interpret your narrative within this expanded framework?

Embodying the climax of my journey, this chapter symbolizes not just a shift in style and expression, but a profound rebirth. Like a canvas turned upside down, it expands our vistas, inviting fresh creativity and mindful engagement. This rebirth transcends the mere physical, delving into the metaphysical realms of the fourth and fifth dimensions where creativity knows no bounds and every artistic decision echoes through the vast multiverse.

As the final brushstrokes settle upon this canvas of my story, understand that this is not the end but merely an elevation—a point from which we gaze not at closure, but at the vibrant potential that 'Elevating Your Life' and 'Reimagining The Nexus of Art' present.

Let this not be a conclusion but an enduring echo, a reverberation of creativity and resilience that lingers in silence, questioning, challenging, and inviting us all to continue the ascent with our tapestries of life ever unfurling. This is our collective crescendo, not ceasing but awaiting—the invitation remains, ever-present, ever-inspiring, for us to ignite and extend without a vanishing point.

A Seat at The Last Supper of My Olde Life

In shadows deep, my journey unfolds,
From the abyss, where negativity molds.

A mental enigma, goals held in strife,
A seat at the last supper of my olde life.

An opportunity, a knock on the door,
Curiosity piqued, skeptic no more.
Generosity in words, a course to untwine,
Sabotaging doubts, a chance to realign.

Mentor's program, a resolve takes hold,
Mindset riddles cracked; stories unfold.
Nomad travels, comfort zones outgrown,
Brittle barriers shattered; strength is shown.

Creativity sparked, flashes ignite,
Frustration transformed, demands for light.
Meditation's embrace, a new sight's born,
The real me knocking, inner door adorned.

A seat at the last supper, old life's retreat,
Venus is reborn, and in creativity, we meet.
No longer in strife, a persuasive speech,
Powerful words, the birth of a new reach.

Through My Brain Fog

Misty thoughts swirl, a foggy veil,
Obscuring thoughts with a hazy trail.
The weight of pain anchors like lead,
A daily trek, where few dare tread.

CRPS, a relentless thief,
Steals the comfort, like a silent grief.

Yet in forgiveness, I find my pace,
Carving a path through this foggy space.

In the midst of the murk, I started to see.
The strength in pain and the will to be free.
Sharper now, with each new dawn,
I face the fog and boldly march on.

Should we all lend an ear, with intent so pure,
And embrace our trials to find a cure?
Grow as a people in understanding and peace,
Offering solace and pain's release.

Let kindness ripple and touch all in its wake,
Fostering healing for humanity's sake.
In unity, we find the light,
Guiding us through the foggiest night.

Rise Higher and Higher!

In the depths of the night, I lay awake.
Muscles tense, mind in a constant ache.
Medicines prescribed, but to no avail.
Sleep, my elusive lover, I continue to trail.

A fall, a diagnosis, a life upturned.
CRPS, frozen shoulder, sleep apnoea churned.
Restless legs, carpal tunnels, and more.
My body was a battleground, at constant war.

No work, no income, a future uncertain.
But I refuse to give up, to draw the curtain.

Mindfulness and art are my weapons of choice.
To find peace within, to hear my inner voice.

I am a student of myself and a willing learner.
To discover my strengths, my passions, and my yearning.
And in sharing my journey, I hope to inspire.
Others to find their light, to rise higher and higher.

The Art of Healing: Leaving a Positive Mark on the Journey of Pain

In life's maze, pain may tread,
A shadow on the path we're led.
Yet in darkness, spirits rise,
Unbound by chains, to claim the prize.

Imagination, a spark ignites,
A beacon in the darkest nights.
#ImaginationIsKey, softly calls,
Guiding through pain's daunting walls.

Art, our refuge, whispers sweet,
#ArtTherapy, solace meet.
Brush in hand, colors bold,
#PaintingMySymptoms, stories told.

CRPS casts its daunting shade,
But #CRPSWarriors, unafraid.
#RaisingCRPSAwareness, light we send,
In unity, our strength won't bend.

Mindfulness, steady, sure,
#MindfulnessGuides, hearts pure.
#GratitudeJournal, grace we find,
In pain's grasp, our souls aligned.

As we navigate pain's tempestuous tide,
Our hashtags stand, side by side.
Each a triumph, each a hope,
A testament to the spirit's scope.

So, let's leave our mark, my friend,
On this pain journey, where we ascend.
With resilience, courage, and art,
We find healing, hope, a fresh start.

What I call #MetaHashtagMuseVerse (join me on X @MetaHashtagMuse)

#BreakYourMouldAndTakeFlight

#BreakingYourMould
#multipledisabilitiesmeeting
#facingmultiplechoices
#navigatingmultiplecomplexities
#uncoveringmultiplereasons
#multipleemotionsembracing
#defyingmultiplelabels
#claimingmultiplerights
#spreadingmultipleawareness
#suturesandbandaidsarenotthehealers
#smokeandmirrorspiercing

#spokeinthewheelturning
#aspiringriseabove
#standtallenduring
#fosteringsharedequality
#digdeepersearching
#eliminatefearandhostilityconquering
#seeitdoesntmatterhowwepaintapicture
#paintitdoesntmatterhowwecolourthepicture
#colouritdoesntmatterhowweseethepicture
#thereisalwaysabiggerpicturerevealing
#highlightingdisabilityabusechronicpainmentalhealthmatters
#championingstandforequality
#cultivatingapositivemindset
#upholdingfreedomtolivewithequalrights
#amplifyingadvocacyagainstpain
#applyingsuturesandbandaidsforunderstanding
#healfromwithininspiring
#mindfulselfredesignchoices
#creativemindfulresilience
#strengthincreativity
#useyourvoiceempowering
#exposemytruth
#crpscreativechooseday
#creativecopingbeyondpain
#alwaysmethodinmymadness
#itshiddeninplainsight
#kindnessandcompassionleading
#BreakYourMouldandtakeflight

Figure 1: Elevate Yor New Beginning (Grayscale version)

Figure 2: #ArtfulnowDigital Can you draw me?

“Your mind shines brightest when you enlighten others; your heart, when you encourage others; your soul, when you elevate others; and your life, when you empower others.”

~ Matshona Dhliwayo

CHAPTER SEVEN

What Life Isn't

By Sharee Siva

When I was a young child, perhaps six or seven years of age, I would, with a child's mind, contemplate, "What makes me 'me?'" A question of who I am, at an age that we begin to identify with ourselves as separate. We begin to develop an identity of ourselves and where we fit in relation to others. A collection of impressions and memories that begin to shape and form our beliefs, values, and who we think we are. This is where the illusion begins. Perhaps my life's path was destined to one day feel so broken, traumatized, and disillusioned that I would be forced to embark on a healing journey, to try to peel back the layers and rediscover who I was. I discovered my true essence, that is life; to elevate our lives, we first need to understand what life is, or rather what life is not.

Part I – Dance with the Devil

At twenty-one, I met a tall, dark, handsome, charming, fun, energetic, and charismatic man from the East. He had no fear, which gave me the impression of authenticity. He wore the "Om" (or "Aum") symbol as a necklace and introduced me to Eastern philosophy. We would talk for hours, and he would listen intently. We became close friends, and the progression of our relationship seemed natural. I thought I had met someone with spiritual knowledge and wisdom, someone I could share life with, love, nurture, and learn from each other. Prior to intimacy, however, he sat me down for a serious talk. He demanded my commitment and said it was "all or nothing." My intuition spoke of a foreboding, but I didn't listen.

"There are those that think that they will never be a victim of abuse, and there are those that know that it can happen to anyone."
Safe Home, SBS

An abuser doesn't punch you (metaphorically) on the first date. The abuse was subtle and insidious, almost imperceptible, the planting of seeds in my mind, a slow brainwashing of sorts. Shrewd contempt, criticism, and invalidation were creeping in at every opportunity. I often felt something was really amiss, but I couldn't quite discern what it was. I often felt confused. I didn't yet know that I was in a relationship with a malevolent manipulator.

Our relationship progressed and the entanglement became greater. We had started a business together and had two beautiful daughters. I believed we were a team, working together to create a shared future of our dreams. There were happy times, and I felt reasonably content. At each stage, however, the abuse notched up a level. My self-confidence and aspirations were slowly eroded by shrewd and underhanded contempt, criticism, and invalidation, which was creeping in at every opportunity.

Time progressed, and it became apparent that we were not a team working towards shared goals; I was, in fact, in a relationship with an individual whose sense of self was that of being superior to all. With a sense of entitlement, together with a lack of respect and empathy, he would manipulate me and others to control and influence outcomes for his own benefit. Self-interest was the only driving force. Lies, deceit, and cheating were the norm. Conflict, gaslighting, and guilt-tripping were common tactics.

Ten years into the relationship, I knew what I was dealing with and I was afraid to leave for many reasons. When my daughters were nine and twelve, the fear of them learning that this was normal became greater. I spoke to him of my unhappiness and he laughed at me. Two weeks later, I wrote him a letter telling him it was over.

What followed were the most difficult seven years of my life. Despite that he had moved on and found a new partner within three months, it took five years to disentangle our financial and family affairs. Many false accusations were made against me, feigned with concern.

This almost destroyed me. His abuse was always hidden behind closed doors, and many people bought into his false accusations and stories; my standing up for what was right and attempting to speak my truth did me no favors. I was perceived as cruel for ending our relationship. He had garnered support from many. I had no voice in the relationship, and now I felt like I also had no voice outside of the relationship. I felt completely alone and isolated.

~~~

Please put the screwdriver down (whilst you're yelling at me)? I feel threatened. "How dare you feel threatened? This is what you think
~~~

of me; you have no idea; your conclusions about me are wrong; I think you are going mad."

~~~

"Can't you see that my actions are a direct result of your actions? I found out that you went to see a lawyer, instead of talking to me! I didn't steal [a very large sum of money], I just wanted it with me. I didn't like how you were spending our money!"

~~~

"My buying a Maserati had nothing to do with receiving a letter from your lawyer the day before. You are crazy the way you link things together."

~~~

"I locked you out of all of the accounts because I was scared—I didn't know what you were going to do next."

~~~

"I want to curl up and die. You misunderstand everything about me. Stop with the lawyers. You call me a thief, but you are capable of murder!"

~~~

"You are not teaching our girls how to behave for their husbands!"

~~~

"If you do that again, I will [insert punishment]."

~~~

"The problem with the world is that fools and fanatics are always so certain of themselves, and wiser people so full of doubts."
Bertrand Russell

~~~

I saw the shapeshifting, the various body language of leaning in, lowering his voice, or standing staunchly upright, with arms crossed. The arrogant sitting back in the chair with legs crossed and palms clasped whilst asserting his superiority and dominance. Facial movements that could quickly move from the sad, quivering bottom lip of a victim whom I was destroying to a broad smile designed to charm. To an expression of shock at any truth spoken to him. Stand-over tactics with anger and taunting, and if I reacted, a satisfied smirk would follow. All were accompanied by well-articulated words designed to dominate, convince, doubt, and confuse. He did always say he should have been an actor or a lawyer.

A wolf in sheep's clothing, and once I saw it, I couldn't un-see it—a manipulator who could lie, cheat, and steal and somehow manage to make it all seem like it was my fault. I realized, for the first time, that our entire relationship was a fraud from start to finish. I felt like the very person who was meant to love me unconditionally had, instead, fed off me like a parasite, draining my love, kindness, and compassion, my happiness and creativity, and replacing it with his anger, guilt, and shame. How could this happen to me? His voice replayed in my mind over and over, in essence saying, "You are not good enough."

Trauma is fracturing. My confidence was shattered. Sometimes, I was too afraid to step outside, fearful, confused, and mistrusting. I felt like the ground beneath me was unstable, always shifting. I couldn't interact with people. Traffic and loud noises sent me into an anxious spin. I no longer trusted myself. I procrastinated. I did not know how to move forward. But I was determined to rise above it.

The Alchemist

In my heart, I know the truth.
In my heart, I know the pain.
I know your pain for you have transferred it to me,
I will transform it into love.

I know what is coming,
the fire burns brightly,
the breeze carries free,
the flow of life becomes like water,
the return to earth where flowers can grow.

Part II – Elevate Your Life

"For a seed to achieve its greatest expression,
it must first come completely undone.

The shell cracks, its insides come out, and everything changes. To someone who doesn't understand growth, it would look like complete destruction."
Cynthia Occelli

Many survivors of abuse are tortured by rumination, mentally reliving the events, the mind attempting to somehow make sense of what had happened. Nothing made sense to me anymore. Everything that I had given meaning to had seemingly collapsed and had been replaced with pain, anger, guilt, blame, shame, and, at times, self-pity.

It was unbearable and I made a conscious choice to disappear from life as I knew it, for I knew that the only way out was to go within. An internal deep dive into the abyss. I went back to the basic question that I began with, "What makes me 'me?'" A question that can only be answered by oneself. I rediscovered and reconnected with the internal essence of life, creation itself, that which precedes our thoughts, our self-identity, and our ego.

Life in its purest form becomes masked over the years by layers of conditions and memories that create the identity we have built. Our ego is somewhat of a trap, governing our view of the world around us, our thoughts and emotions, and our reactions to outside stimuli. Our ego becomes our suit of armor, layers of protection that can distort our view and experience of life.

A space or a gap exists between creation and the knowledge of your own existence. This is where life resides, and it is the same creation that resides in not only each and every one of us but the entirety of existence. Healing is a journey of peeling back the layers, and it is not a linear path. Sometimes two steps forward and then ten back, sometimes peeling a layer, only to create another layer of a different color! It is a lifelong journey. Our egoic sense of self holds on tightly. It is a deep inquiry that takes strength and courage, but I discovered along the way that nothing can break my soul, not even death.

I believe we all have some recognition that there is something miraculous in all of us, a life that we cannot easily or logically define. It's a process of paying attention to creation itself and bringing it into our conscious awareness to practice residing in this "space" or "gap," creating a distance between creation and you. In this space resides truth and love, and there is nothing to fear. Everything else is an illusion of our own making. We are creation itself, and the process of elevating life is not so much about becoming something; it is a process of unbecoming everything we think we know.

The eternal essence of life, consciousness in its
purest form, a space within us that is
infinite and ever-expanding.
To know, feel, and perceive this, even momentarily,
is the foundation for which we can begin to elevate life.
For life supports life, it is creation itself that connects us all.
The universe, including ourselves, is in a constant
state of motion, subtly vibrating,
in perfect balance and harmony.
Our essence is love, creation itself.

"Nothing real can be threatened.
Nothing unreal exists.

Herein lies the peace of God."
~ A Course in Miracles

~~~

Here are some of what I discovered in my journey to elevate my life.

Responsibility

What I struggled with overcoming the most was the intentional degradation of my self-worth, the intentional exploitation of what I could provide for him, and, if he made any mistakes, the distortion of the truth to shift all blame to me. If I chose not to accept any blame, he then reverted from bully to victim, and I was labeled as a destroyer or a murderer. All to validate him and protect his own bubble, ego, or self-identification of being superior?

We all make mistakes, but an inability to own them destroys those around us. It felt particularly cruel and it has been a long journey of recovery for me. The upside is that I had a first-hand lesson in *what not to be*. Everything that was taken away from me became so valuable that it became the internal driving force to elevate my life.

"Anyone who fights with monsters should make sure that he does not in the process become a monster himself. And when you look for a long time into an abyss, the abyss also looks into you."
Friedrich Nietzche
~~~

It is true that the people who hurt you the most are your best teachers. At one point, I realized that by remaining stuck in the pain, anger, fear, and blame that I felt, I was actually not that different from him. A poison that resided in a place of my egoic false self that needed to protect and defend who I thought myself to be. We mistake our psychological drama for life, and I did not want to be this way. I didn't want to live like a victim. Additionally, I knew if I didn't clear it, I, too, was susceptible to perpetuating the cycle.

~~~

While the past cannot be changed, I learned that we need not define ourselves by it. We can take full responsibility for ourselves in the present moment and grow from it.

Ultimately, our life was ignited singularly and alone at the time of inception, and we will leave this body in the same way. It is unlikely that someone will volunteer to come with you at the time of death! Everything that happens in between is your responsibility; it's all you. The illusion of yourself that has been created is all your own doing.

Recognition of this opens us to the possibility that we, alone, can fix it. Most of us have experienced psychological or emotional wounds at some point in our lives, but ultimately, it is our choice to become bitter or better. We can all end the cycle of 'hurt people hurt people'. The buck stops with our selves, and we must heal ourselves first. Is it not the ultimate responsibility to heal ourselves and elevate our own life, which in turn elevates all life?

Along the way, I discovered an alternate way to look at the word "responsibility," breaking it down into two parts as our ability to
~~~

respond. This puts us back in the driving seat of our own lives, and instead of reacting to external forces or stimuli, we can pause and take charge. Sometimes, this can be difficult if you find yourself on the receiving end of false accusations and anger! It takes practice to become aware of your responses.

BK Shivani, a motivational speaker and spiritual mentor, in a recording of one of her events, titled "Love Yourself, Release the Hurt," eloquently shares some simple guidance on our ability to respond. Shivani begins with an example of a glass. One person describes the glass as beautiful—it is silver, it is a marvelous vessel for it holds my water, and so on. The next person, looking at the same glass, may say it is terrible, too small, lacks color, and so forth. The same glass, two perspectives. She goes on to say that in the person's ability to appreciate the glass, they are talking about themselves and their own quality to see beauty in things.

Not everyone will appreciate you and see the beauty in you! People's opinions of you and behavior towards you can and will fluctuate. If a person says something hurtful (let's say, "You are so stupid, you have no idea about anything,") do we have a right to feel hurt? How dare he say that to me? And our mind goes on and replays it, and later, we may even think of the perfect response: Oh, I should have said that back! Have you ever done that?

BK Shivani shares with us the simple truth: three options on how we can *choose* to respond when someone projects *their* negativity onto us. First, we can throw it back to the person, say something equally, if not more hurtful, and reflect their negativity back to them. The second option is to absorb the negativity, keep quiet, and not respond—a little better than the first, but silently in our mind, we continue the drama and hurt. How dare he, and so on. The third and desired option is that when they hit us with their pain, we take charge of our mind and protect ourselves from the hurt; we transform it and radiate love and respect back to them.

In the relationship, I had done a lot of absorbing! Once you absorb it, it requires a lot of effort to transform the pain into love. Reflecting the same back and absorbing only adds pain to the pain. If one person is in pain in any situation, very soon the infection of pain is with everybody—the family, the work environment, etc. When everyone is in pain, the person who shared their pain becomes in more pain; it's a vicious cycle.

Likewise, it takes only one person to transform and heal the pain, one person to take responsibility for healing themselves. You can choose to be that person. Trauma is not what happens to us but how we respond to it. It really is a tough lesson to learn.

Boundaries

Taking a moment to re-center yourself, to find the space and reside in pure awareness before compulsively responding to what people may be throwing at you, is a lesson in self-love and boundaries. It is not about people pleasing, which I was prone to! It simply protects you from the entanglement. You are not responsible for changing, fixing, or regulating another person's emotions or sense of self. Remind yourself that people's behavior and choices in life, what they say or do, is on them; it's not about you, so stop absorbing other people's pain and recognize what belongs to you and what doesn't.

Radiating love and respect back to them is equally not about them! It's about choosing to love and respect yourself enough that you will not give your power away freely by allowing someone else to determine who you think you are.

Just because another has created a certain reality for themselves and is attempting to draw you in does not mean you must participate. Keep your karma clean and have the strength and courage to walk away, without guilt, fear, or shame, from people, situations, or structures designed to discriminate, diminish, or restrict your self-determination. You cannot do another individual's work for them.

Conversely, the internalization of external positive validation will inevitably lead to the internalization of negativity. The pendulum swings both ways, but to maintain recognition of your own inherent worth is to recognize that everything is an expression of the other person. This also represents an opportunity to radiate love. Everything that you need is within you.

Focus on Yourself

Stay in your own lane and focus on yourself, not others. Life doesn't discriminate; my life, your life, and everything around me are life, manifested in different densities. Life is creation itself and we are all connected. The air we breathe is a subtle interaction with the life of trees. It is all happening in harmony, with little effort or conscious awareness.

Once you see this, equality is a natural consequence. Your gender, race, religion, intellect, wealth, or beauty, or lack thereof, depending upon the illusion of separateness you have created for yourself, does not make you more than or less than, above or below anyone. If you feel that it does make you superior to anyone, it is the beginning of the delusion of not seeing reality as it is, and you need to check in with yourself, take a long look into the mirror, and polish the view! It is this certainty of one's own self, a small and insular view of life, where feelings of jealousy, envy, hate, power, and greed arise. Ideologies that are the source of all exploitation, crime, and war in the world.

Competition or comparison with others is only limiting the possibilities of yourself. There will be someone wealthier than you, more beautiful than you, or smarter than you. Money can be lost, external beauty fades, and intellect can dissolve into dementia! You may not even be alive tomorrow. Circumstances change; life is not a comparison, a competition, or a race; it is creation in motion. Even in competitive sports or the like, if you focus only on your opponent, you may not discover your own full potential and capabilities. We are all different; respect each other's differences and capabilities and focus on being your best version.

Empathy, Love, and Compassion

The most difficult obstacle I faced was understanding empathy and compassion. I often put other people's needs above mine out of a false sense of empathy and a desire to protect other people or not hurt other people's feelings. It was a button that was pushed regularly, for it usually worked. It was really destructive to me, as my kindness was viewed as a weakness to be exploited. I felt that the very essence of myself was being used against me. I refused to become anything else but compassionate; I just needed to better understand what it meant.

Empathy is the foundation and internal compass of love; the very emotion that glues us together as human beings, and it's the ability to understand how another person may feel. It is not to be confused with giving and doing for others. It comes back to responsibility—you cannot do the work for another, and if you continue to do so, you are removing the very lessons they may need to take responsibility and grow. You can only love another to the extent that you love yourself, and self-love knows when to have boundaries.

Relationships are not a negotiation or transactional process of extracting what you need and desire from another person. If you enter relationships with the expectation that you will have certain needs met, they are bound for disaster. Allow people to be who they are and show you who they are. Use discernment about who you allow to access you.

You have everything you need already. Relationships require a willingness to share everything you are, nurture, and elevate life for yourself and others without expecting to get something in return.

Two Sides of the Same Coin

Awareness of your true self allows reality to be seen just as it is. There becomes nothing to judge, attach to, or give meaning to. We strive for what is important to us, and of course, we want pleasantness and well-being, but everything becomes life in motion. Experiences of "good" or "bad," "right" and wrong become less relevant. Everything is just happening. We are the coin, the center, and the sides united as one experience.

Our ability to deal with difficult situations becomes much stronger, and negative emotions arise, but the attachment to them reduces; everything comes and goes, and this too shall pass.

Forgiveness

Occasionally, people with good intentions, who wanted the best for me, would say, "Just let it go" or "forgive and forget." Others became impatient with me for my inability to let it go and move on. Healing takes time, and while in the abyss that is trauma, the idea of forgiveness can sometimes feel like rubbing salt into the wound.

I wanted the pain and the injustice of how I was treated to be acknowledged and sometimes even punished. I now feel that if I had just let it go or forgiven and forgotten, I may have missed the valuable lessons and even repeated the same mistakes. My very nature is not to let go; my nature is to become so involved, I need to work it out, which takes time. No one can rush your healing, not even you; show yourself compassion and do not expect yourself to be anything but what you are today. It's a process of acceptance, responsibility, and a choice to become wounded or wise.

Forgiveness, at the time, felt like excusing and accepting the behavior or absolving any wrongdoing, which I was unwilling to do. My understanding of forgiveness, however, has changed, and I believe that the word is used and interpreted somewhat inaccurately. Forgiveness is for yourself; it is the process of elevating to a new level of understanding, growing, and changing to the point where you recognize that what happened was in the realms of your knowledge at that time. You didn't know what you didn't know.

Essentially, there becomes nothing to forgive. The story no longer matters. It is a point in growth when you no longer suffer the memory of the past and start living wholeheartedly in the present.

~~~

"And those who were seen dancing were thought to be insane by those who couldn't hear the music."
Freidrich Nietzche

~~~

Paint Your Own Life

We see something as a particular color, not because what we are looking at is that color; it is what it gives away or reflects. We see red not because it is red; rather, it holds back everything that white light contains and reflects red. In the same way, you can live your life choosing what to absorb and what to reflect. Choose your color and paint your life!

We have much more inner strength and power than we know. A determined and intense focus on the self, free from illusion, a space to reside, can unlock immense strength and power. It is a boundless space of infinite knowledge and wisdom. Set yourself free, unlock the cage, and elevate your life, for you yourself hold the key.

“You get tested the most when it’s time for you to elevate."

~ Unknown

CHAPTER EIGHT

Transcendence: Embodying the Divine Within

By Mariese B. Vacalares

The Call to Transcendence

We are entering a new era of humanity's spiritual journey into higher consciousness. Since the recent pandemic, everything has been changing, and we are seeking balance and equilibrium where order arises out of chaos. We are experiencing a rebirth and witnessing a great shift from the old to the new, from individual to planetary consciousness, transcending the human experience, Awakening to the Divine within, and Ascending to a Higher Truth and Reality with our True Identity. With that, I look forward with much hope to the days when there is less separation or fragmentation and more oneness, unity, peace, and harmony among us.

There was a time in my life when I felt so unsettled and bored doing the same personal and business routine over and over, even with life's little pleasures sprinkled in. Feeling stuck and fed up, I literally thought loudly in my mind while driving home, "STOP BEING HUMAN!" The words came out like a bomb, and I thought, "Whoah, what does that mean?!" as I pulled over by the roadside.

It took me over a decade to understand what the phrase meant, but later, I realized it meant to just "START BEING DIVINE!" Then began my journey for this shift in consciousness from the human to the Divine, searching and yearning for deeper meaning and connection in my life.

When the pandemic started in March 2020, I had the opportunity to shift consciousness. The initial feeling was akin to having a rug pulled from under your feet and then falling with nothing to hold on to. I felt helpless, with only my aging parents with me in the house. We didn't let our household staff in as some had become sick; they came only by the gate to bring food, medicine, or information.

We endured more than a year and a half being locked up. Still, thanks to the advancement in technology and the Knowledge Industry, I was wired to the internet and connected with all the powers out there who continued to thrive and help raise humanity's consciousness amid the pandemic.

So began my journey to self-introspection: I was locked up and connected with many online groups—business, personal development, socio-civic, and especially spiritual groups. I read books and articles and attended webinars through Zoom with my parents.

It was a special moment in my life where I had an intimate bond with my parents, doing household chores together, "specialized" early morning exercises at the rooftop for the precious sun exposure, early morning and late afternoon Agnihotra (an ancient Indian ritual to purify the atmosphere as far as a radius of twenty kilometers away), and reading and praying the Holy Rosary day and night.

I was looking at my own self-transcendence together with my parents—at rising above or going beyond our limits and boundaries. With the spiritual teachings we received from books, articles, and the Zoom webinars we attended with our spiritual group of light bearers and torchbearers, we increased our awareness of accessing higher levels of consciousness and existence.

We could find shifts in our perspective and connect with deeper truths, universal principles, and Divine realities beyond the limitations of the ego or our personal identity. This process of transcendence led us to experience unity, interconnectedness, and spiritual enlightenment, enabling us to perceive reality from a broader perspective.

My family, including my father Salvador, mother Vilma, sister Sara who came home in March 2021, and myself, were able to attend weekly meetings for the seminars held online and know the truth of the "Mighty I Am Presence," our True Identity. We had lively conversations over dinner about the topics and uncommon truths we discovered that we hadn't usually heard about.

Conversations about Ascension, or how to ascend, were becoming common in my conversations with my father. We did our daily prayers together in the morning and late afternoon. Perhaps our frequency and vibration were raised to the highest level possible by this time with the help of the hierarchies of heaven as we prayed.

In 2020, I found myself trapped in my environment but with a heightened awareness of the human limitations we have been enduring for centuries. We have been holding on to our human ego for so long, preventing us from seeing our own True Reality. With the new knowledge I received, I was able to perceive grander things to do for myself and for others.

I was looking forward to creating other methods for wellness and organizing groups to help improve our human condition, starting in my own locality. I had the chance to put my thoughts and ideas in writing when I contributed a chapter entitled "Oneness in Leadership" for *The Way of the Leader,* published in 2021 as the twenty-fourth installment in the Journey of Riches series.

But then my family got sick in September 2021 and I lost focus, trying to help them heal with all types of healing modalities. Eventually, my parents passed away in a span of two years, my Dad in 2021 and my Mom last year, 2023. I needed to get back on track and raise my frequency and vibration from this downward spiral as I dealt with feeling stressed, distracted, unfocused, and unwell.

Understanding the Human Experience

The human condition is intricate, marked by a tapestry of desires, fears, and limitations. Desires propel us forward, urging us to seek fulfillment and meaning, yet they can also ensnare us in cycles of craving and attachment. Fears, born from vulnerability and uncertainty, often hinder our growth, trapping us in patterns of avoidance and stagnation. Whether physical, emotional, or societal, limitations constrain our potential, compelling us to confront our mortality and finitude.

Common struggles and challenges emerge on the path to transcendence, testing our resolve and resilience. The ego, driven by self-preservation and identity, resists dissolution, clinging to familiar narratives and constructs. Inner conflicts arise as we confront the shadows within, navigating the depths of our psyche with courage and compassion. External pressures, shaped by societal norms and expectations, impose conformity and compliance, obscuring the truth of our authentic selves.

Yet amidst these trials, opportunities for growth and transformation abound. Through introspection and self-awareness, we unravel the layers of conditioning and illusion, uncovering the essence of our being. Surrender becomes a portal to transcendence as we relinquish control and surrender to the flow of existence. Connection with ourselves and the Divine becomes a source of solace and inspiration, guiding us toward wholeness and integration.

Essentially, the journey toward transcendence is a profound odyssey marked by paradox and revelation. It invites us to honor the full spectrum of human experience, embracing our vulnerabilities and strengths with humility and grace. As we awaken to the Divine within, we discover that transcendence is not merely a destination but a continuous unfolding of the soul, a sacred dance between the finite and the infinite.

The Quest for Spiritual Awakening

Before I explore the importance of mindfulness, meditation, and self-reflection in expanding consciousness and how these practices helped me resume my journey toward awakening, let me step back before the pandemic and share how my story began.

My story of awakening toward a spiritual path started during my student days when I first got hold of a four-book series entitled *The Lost Teachings of Jesus* by Mark and Elizabeth Prophet. These books unraveled the lost years and teachings of Jesus when he traveled to the East from seventeen to thirty-three years old. They taught about the missing texts on karma and reincarnation and provided missing links to the mysteries of the knowledge of our true identity and the power of our inner Christ. The books recaptured the heart of Jesus's message so that just like Him, we could reconnect with our Divine source to realize our full potential.

After my student days, I slightly forgot the lessons from these Masters' lives until 2007 when I connected online with Dr. Pamela Fernandez, a professor at the University of the Philippines Los Banos. We attended a national conference in 2006 for the Anthroposophical group and discussed the effects of elementals on nature while reflecting on recurring drowning incidents in our area.

After reconnecting with Dr. Pam, I revived my research on elementals and sent her a few copies of articles from *St. Germain on Alchemy* by Mark and Elizabeth Prophet. I continued researching other issues and found more articles and sources about the Ascended Masters. Dr. Pam and I continued exchanging what we had found and discussed what was being birthed from our research and communication.

So, I credited our communication with pushing me to further research and updating my knowledge on the Ascended Masters and their teachings and also on the practice of Agnihotra—the healing fire from the ancient science of Ayurveda.

The book I read about St. Germain dumbfounded me earlier since mid-2000. I could not easily digest and assimilate the thought of the past embodiments of St. Germain, which included St. Joseph, St. Alban, Christopher Columbus, Merlin the Magician, the scientist

Roger Bacon, and Francis Bacon—who authored the Shakespearean plays.

According to another source, the Ascension-Research website, Saint Germain was also embodied as Plato, Prophet Samuel, High Priest on Atlantis, and Ruler of a Golden Age civilization thousands of years ago.

He is the prime Ascended Being to oversee the next 2000 years, often called the Age of Aquarius. The next era is in our hands, as we, beings in embodiment, have the authority to decide the future of Earth. But if we work on it and call on St. Germain for his help, support, guidance, and direction, with his power and authority, we together can manifest a new era, a new Golden Age, along with the Angels and the Hierarchy of Heaven.

During the pandemic, I began to read or re-read the books that I had bought, including that unread since twenty years ago and did research on the internet to satisfy my longing for spiritual fulfillment. I delved into the inherent human desire for transcendence and how it manifests in various aspects of life, from seeking purpose and meaning to exploring existential questions—Who am I? Why am I here? Where did I come from? Where am I going? What is my purpose in Life? These questions were getting answered when I began my own research, though more questions were yet to be answered as I continued along with my Quest.

I remembered these books discussing the Masquerade we are all in and the need to unmask our Real Self. The books talked about Kal-Desh and the illusion of time and space, about Momentum, and the Ascended Masters.

I started researching the many groups that studied Ascended Master teachings. One of the most popular was founded by authors Mark and Elizabeth Prophet, who became the Messengers for the Ascended Masters. I just found out this year that Mark Prophet ascended himself as the Ascended Master Lanello in the 1970s (with famous past embodiments such as Noah builder of the Ark, Lot of Sodom and Gomorrah, Aesop, Bodhidharma, Amenhotep, Lancelot, Saladin, Hiawatha) leaving behind his wife Elizabeth to continue their mission until she passed away.

At that time, I had already found several groups that studied the Ascended Masters, but later, one stood out: the Temple of the Presence in Arizona, where another couple, Monroe Julius Shearer and Carolyn Louise Shearer, were trained to lead as the new Messengers beginning in 1995. Here, new messages from the Ascended Masters for the New Dispensation were received and relayed by Carolyn and Monroe as live dictations and discourses.

The Story of the Godhead Charioteers, by the Anointed Representatives Monroe Julius and Carolyn Louise Shearer, described the Ascended Masters as "humans who have completed their journey as the Godhead Charioteers and attained the Ascension in the Light. They are our Elder Brothers and Sisters who have gone before us on this Path and returned victoriously back into Oneness with their Higher Selves. They could master the forces of nature within themselves and become Immortal Beings of Light who left a record of their mastery for us to follow."

Examples of the Ascended Masters who walked among us include the Beloved Jesus, Mother Mary, Gautama Buddha, Saint Germain, El Morya, Kuthumi, Krishna and the Goddess of Liberty. More recent examples include Godfre Ray King, Lanello, Mother Teresa, Pope John Paul II, and many others.

Embracing the Divine Within

Looking back on my foundations with yoga as a student at the Art of Living Foundation in 2008 with teacher Julie Ang and later certified in 2019 as a yoga teacher in her One Yoga studio with teacher Anna Carbonell, I consider yoga one tool for embracing the Divine within. Seeking to connect with something greater than ourselves, we explore more possibilities in our pursuit of a purposeful and fulfilling life.

Movement and yoga practices are crucial in enhancing this connection as we learn to move consciously and mindfully, bringing awareness to each breath and posture. As we feel and listen to our bodies and energies, more deeply heightening our awareness, we create a bridge between our physical and spiritual planes.

This connection between body, mind, and spirit helps us become more familiar with our physical being and better understand our personal experiences. Increasing this connection with Divine timing, we can witness a beautiful transformation of spirit into the physical realm. We embark on a journey of self-discovery and spiritual growth as we embrace the path of embodiment through movement and yoga, and over time, we realize our body is a sacred vessel where our Divine essence resides.

I was taught to embrace and embody the Divine within, realizing my True Identity as a Child of God. Being in Oneness with our

Higher Self, the Christ Self or Divine nature sets the tone for a glorious and blessed life.

"Seek ye first the Kingdom of God and his righteousness; and all these things shall be added unto you!"
— Matthew 6:33

It is our responsibility to take care of our bodies as the Temple of the Living God and heed the call to follow Jesus Christ as he walked on the earth as the Way, the Truth, and the Life. Following Jesus is to put on the mantle of Christ's Consciousness.

Our Divine destiny is to fulfill the goal of the Ascension and elevate our lives into Christhood.

Transcending Ego and Illusion

Times have truly changed, and the rules of the game have changed. Even money as we know it is not what it used to be. They say the new currency isn't bitcoin, it's attention! In this modern world, attention is the new money and your personal brand is the bank. Building that one Personal Brand that stands out on social media, which is portable and relatable, is the new trend for freedom, be it for time and space or for financial freedom.

When it comes to freedom, perhaps our ego is leading us toward material freedom rather than the kind of freedom that is eternal. I later found out that this matters most when we get to the spiritual part of ascension, aligning with our true self. Here comes the issue of identity: whether we choose to hold on to our outer mask or get rid of it to attune with our real self.

According to Mark Prophet, the wholly perfect Divine creation of God needs to be revealed by unmasking the fake human creation that we ignorantly hold on to. The ego has helped us discover many beautiful things about ourselves. In the initial stages of identity development, the ego represents the will to be and maintains some sense of self-worth until the soul itself attains the strength and desire for self-transcendence.

At this point, the soul is now willing for the Divine ego to supersede the lesser human ego when the lesser sense of selfhood is no longer needed to sustain the finite awareness. When the human ego becomes so rigid that it becomes frozen in time—and this rigidity will be its ultimate undoing—its only chance of survival will be its displacement by the Divine filament of being.

Living in Alignment with the Divine

Through the years I studied different methods for self-transcendence including music(classical, instrumental), dance (NIA, Zumba), movement (martial arts, qigong, yoga), scientific prayers (calls, fiats, decrees, mantras, chants), altered states (alpha -Silva Method and Theta Healing), wellness(WILDFIT), journalling, book writing, coaching, spiritual affirmations, nature treks.

Early this year, I found a lot of synchronicity as I began adopting a fresher outlook on life. I started connecting with a global and local group of positive people—coaches, mentors, leaders, influencers, entrepreneurs, teachers, light bearers, and dreamers. I started with online courses and even live and online seminars and an outdoor farm retreat, all pointing me to get back on track and embrace self-care and self-love, prioritizing self-growth while equipping myself with the tools, skills, resources, methodologies, and strategies needed before I went out to battle and "Save the World."

My Facebook post in mid-January became funny and synchronous as I wrote on my wall, "First off for 2024 is to learn to FLY—First Love Yourself." My Facebook Avatar acted out my message, wearing a beaming face for the New Year before hiding under a box with a rainbow at the top of the backdrop and then popping up and flying toward the front, carrying a gift box.

The post looked fantastic with the flying avatar, and one of my coaches said it was an incredible resolution for the New Year. While most people were looking forward and outward, I was trying to look inward for solutions. Perhaps that set the tone for my quest and goals this year.

As the year 2024 unfolded, I found myself in all kinds of groups and events—Inner World Tribe with Hui Hui and Martin, Ignite House with Wellness Angel Joana and founder Andre, Take off Summit with CEO Joana and Jev, Theta Healing group for Soulmates and Self-Love with Sanaiyah, Wildfit lifestyle with Coach Glory Jane, Extreme Sales Maximizer with Coach Brylle, Pandemic Proof System with Coach JM, Inspirepreneur by Coach JC, Attraction Marketing with Coach JP, Unmessable with Coach Aljur, Time to Rise with Tony Robbins, Ascended Masters Class on Advancements In Christianity in the 21st Century by the Temple of the Presence Philippines. All these groups point me back to developing the self-love and self-growth needed to achieve self-transcendence, preparing me before I go out to serve the world, my community, and my environment.

It is important to embody the Christ Consciousness as Jesus did, living the Way, the Truth, and the Life as Jesus taught. The latest live dictation through the Messenger Carolyn Shearer of the resurrected and ascended Jesus Christ was recently shared on March 30, 2024. The message spoke of "the importance of placing our attention upon the Christ, our own Holy Christ Presence, and of becoming that Christ - the Christ-in-Action. It is important for the Sons and Daughters of God to Awaken to the Truth of their Identity, for they are sloughing off the best of what they could possibly achieve in this incarnation, for they have turned their back upon the opportunities extended to them."

The Journey Continues

The journey of self-transcendence and spiritual awakening is ongoing and ever-evolving. We can embrace this adventure with openness, curiosity, and courage as we move through ups and downs along the way. With patience, humility, and resilience, we can develop the momentum to embrace the process of transcendence. We can find sources for further exploration, such as books, podcasts, or spiritual communities, to support us in our continued journey of growth and transformation.

Receiving new messages from sages and saints that we know of in popular history is quite exhilarating. Still, I feel it's such a waste that only a few of us are aware of them or open to listening to their new messages. The Ascended Masters, angels, and the hierarchy of Heaven want to reach out to mankind to offer their help and assistance to get us out of this rut we are in—which is our own doing, the karma of mankind's ignorance and rebellion against the Truth of God, thus causing the enduring separation.

For eons, they have patiently waited. However, time and space don't exist in their heavenly abode, for individuals willing to do the Will of God, take up the cross, follow the path of Jesus Christ, and gain Christ Consciousness. They look forward to those Sons and Daughters of God who can master the art and science of the Ascended Master Way of Life.

The Ascended Masters are our teachers and guides to our ultimate goal of the Ascension. It is best to learn of the **Ascended Master Way of Life** which encompasses profound spiritual principles and practices that guide seekers toward enlightenment and self-realization. Let's explore some key aspects outlined on the internet :

1. **Inner Transformation:**

    - Inner transformation is the foundation of spiritual growth. This involves self-awareness, self-reflection, and the pursuit of higher consciousness.
    - Practices such as meditation, mindfulness, and contemplation help individuals connect with their inner wisdom and divine essence.

2. **Service to Others:**

    - Ascended Masters exemplify selfless service. They encourage us to extend compassion, kindness and love to others.
    - By helping fellow beings, we align with universal energies and contribute positively to the collective consciousness.

3. **Alignment with Universal Laws:**

   - Ascended Masters emphasize living in harmony with universal laws. These laws govern the cosmos and influence our experiences.
   - Examples include the Law of Attraction (like attracts like), the Law of Cause and Effect (karma), and the Law of Vibration (everything vibrates at a specific frequency).

4. **Transcending Ego:**

   - Egoic desires and attachments hinder spiritual progress. Ascended Masters teach detachment from material possessions and ego-driven desires.
   - By transcending the ego, we open ourselves to higher truths and deeper connections.

5. **Seeking Wisdom and Truth:-**

   - Seekers are encouraged to explore spiritual texts, ancient wisdom, and esoteric knowledge.
   - The pursuit of truth involves questioning, seeking, and discerning what resonates with our soul.

6. **Self-Mastery:**

   - Mastery over one's thoughts, emotions, and actions is essential. Ascended Masters exemplify discipline, patience, and resilience.
   - Through self-mastery, we overcome limitations and align with our divine purpose.

7. Unity Consciousness:

- Ascended Masters recognize the interconnectedness of all life. They promote unity, compassion, and inclusivity.
- When we see beyond individual differences, we embrace unity consciousness.

We can search for a more comprehensive and deeper study of the Ascended Master Way of Life than what is outlined above. It does invite us to explore, learn, and evolve, ultimately leading us toward enlightenment and Oneness with the divine.

Ascended Master El Morya was embodied as the Patriarch Abraham and King Arthur of the Camelot Sagas. He delivered a message on February 2, 1999, published in *The Voice of the Temple*, calling the attention of those who are ready to hear His Voice declaring the unmitigated Truth of the Law, the Reality of the Ascended Masters, and the full and complete Teaching of Cosmic Law in bold, plain, clear language. He spoke of the "demand of the Will of God for the Oneness of each life-stream with their God's Presence.

Whatever it takes to accomplish that goal is the commandment. For some, there will be a greater demand for the transmutation of human conditions. For others, there will be many veils, of illusion and maya that must go into the Flame. For still others, the ego will be the greatest stumbling block, for these are those who fashion themselves knowledgeable in all the ways of the world as experts. They will not be able to return to the pure heart of the child, who is required to bend the knee before their God's presence to detect their spiritual blindness. The lifespan of those in physical embodiment is far too short for anyone to waste precious time. Yet, time and time again, there transpires the same dreary waste and squandering of Light and Opportunity we have seen for countless centuries!

You may continue to read his full message from the website listed below.

I found a message from *Mother Mary on the Light*: "Your Mission begins with you. You cannot save a planet and raise the Light in others until it is raised in your own temple. While you can talk about high ideals and guide a person to this or that, becoming an example is always the greatest teacher. You can ignite those you contact by conserving the Light of the Cosmic Christ within your temple. Then, as you walk, talk, and fulfill your dreams, you will bless all of life wherever you go. This is the Mission. This is the genuine Grail Quest. You hold the goal in your mind. You maintain the Immaculate Concept, but it is in actively pursuing the Quest that you win your victory each day."

For further exploration of these new spiritual principles, we can search the internet, read books, articles, and newsletters, or listen to the live dictations and discourses from the Messengers of the Temple of the Presence (www.templeofthepresence.org) to support our continued journey of growth and transformation.

Awakening to Divine Potential and Embodying Our True Identity

Shifting consciousness from human to Divine, I thought of six levels of elevation: awareness, acceptance, application, amplification, acceleration, and Ascension. Hoping I can work my way up to this realization.

From the guidance of the Holy Spirit or the Maha Chohan, "we need to embody these God qualities, which are the building blocks of the Virtues of Christ such as love, harmony, purity, peace, hope, poise, courage, charity, strength, happiness, patience, faith, humility, fearlessness, and sacred fire. Without embracing these Virtues and allowing the Flame upon the Altar of our Heart to command life's journey, we are just being tossed about by the winds of human consciousness, the water of emotional tides, and the dis-ease that we allow to settle in our own bodies," said the Maha Chohan.

Embodying Divine consciousness involves cultivating a profound shift in our perception and awareness of our Divine nature, allowing us to align with the inherent Divinity within. We accept our True Identity as a Child of God—our Mighty I Am Presence. We apply the laws and practices to accelerate and reach our goal of the Ascension.

Here are some steps to facilitate this transcendent journey:

Practice Self-Reflection and Inner Inquiry: Begin by exploring your inner landscape through meditation, introspection, and contemplation. Reflect on your beliefs, values, and motivations, inquiring into the nature of your true self beyond the egoistic mind.

Cultivate Presence: Practice mindfulness and presence in daily life, anchoring yourself in the present moment. By cultivating awareness of the here and now, you can transcend the limitations of past conditioning and future anxieties, allowing the Divine essence to emerge.

Surrender to the Flow: Release attachment to outcomes and surrender to the natural flow of life. Trust in the universe's wisdom and embrace the inherent perfection of each moment, allowing Divine grace to guide your path.

Cultivate Love and Compassion: Nurture a heart-centered approach to life, embracing love, compassion, and empathy for all beings. Recognize the interconnectedness of all existence and cultivate a deep sense of unity and oneness with the world around you.

Practice Gratitude: Cultivate an attitude of gratitude for the abundance and blessings present in your life. By acknowledging and appreciating the Divine gifts surrounding you, you align yourself with the flow of Divine energy and open yourself to receiving even greater blessings.

Serve Others: Embody the Divine by serving the highest good of all beings. Engage in acts of kindness, generosity, and service, recognizing that by uplifting others, you also uplift yourself and contribute to the collective evolution of consciousness.

Awaken to Your True Nature: Recognize that your essence is inherently Divine and that you express the universal consciousness. Let go of identification with the limited sense of self and awaken to your true nature as an eternal, limitless being.

Integrate Spiritual Practices: Engage in spiritual practices such as meditation, yoga, or scientific prayers like decrees, fiats, calls to the Archangels, Ascended Masters, or Divine Beings to deepen your connection to the Divine. These practices can help quiet the mind, open the heart, and attune you to the subtle realms of life.

By embodying these principles and practices, you can gradually transcend the limitations of the human ego and awaken to the radiant presence of Divine consciousness within you. This journey is one of deepening awareness, surrender, and alignment with the highest truths of existence.

As Nikola Tesla once said, to understand the universe, think in terms of energy, frequency, and vibration. There are wonderful sacred frequencies out there for healing and manifestation.

Here are the lyrics of a song I'm trying to co-create inspired by the theme of transcendence.

Elevate Your Life

[Verse] Rise up from the ashes. Let your spirit take flight. Shifting consciousness to realms where darkness turns to light. Find the truest version of yourself. Shine your light oh so bright.

"When you elevate your thinking ...
You elevate your life."

~ Keith Craft

CHAPTER NINE

Dancing in the Shadows Transforming Grief into Healing and Hope

By Gabriela D Delgadillo

As I eagerly embark on the journey of crafting this chapter, I find myself embraced by the vibrant pulse of springtime in Arizona. Beyond my window, nature conducts a symphony of rebirth, where orange blossoms sway gracefully in the breeze, their fragrant essence a tribute to life's perpetual evolution. The lively chorus of birds and the gentle touch of sunlight remind us of existence's sacred rhythm, where change is constant and every moment holds the potential for metamorphosis.

In the throes of grief, time can seem suspended, trapped in a void of sorrow. Yet, like the seamless transition of seasons, we too can navigate the turbulent waters of loss and emerge renewed and invigorated.

This chapter is a testament to humanity's indomitable spirit, a guiding light for those journeying through the shadows of grief. It extends an embrace to the cosmic wisdom that underscores our transient existence, acknowledging our interconnectedness within the vast fabric of creation. Through a spiritual lens, we discover comfort in the realization that even amidst darkness resides the seed of profound growth and healing, nurtured by the benevolent touch of the Divine.

As we embark on this journey of transformation together, may we find solace in the eternal cadence of the universe and draw upon the reservoir of our inner strength, knowing that the Divine presence is ever near, ready to mend and elevate us in our times of trial. For within the depths of grief lies the seed of transcendence, poised to blossom with the promise of newfound wisdom and unwavering resilience.

Dancing in the Shadows

In the depths of night, amidst a tender embrace of love's light, my departed husband, Nathan, visited me. His presence radiated a comforting glow in the quiet darkness, inviting me into a sacred dance of healing. With his name whispered softly on the breeze, we moved as one, our spirits intertwining in a divine rhythm of solace and remembrance. Grief gave way to a profound sense of peace in that hushed moment, as Nathan's ethereal touch filled the void with love's eternal embrace.

In the shadow of the night, he appeared before me, a gentle presence that transcended the boundaries of this world. As I played our favorite dancing music, I closed my eyes, immersing myself in the melodies that always brought us joy. And there he was, holding me tight, twirling me around gracefully and easily. It was as if he hadn't really left, his spirit finding a way to reach out to me. Though my mind understood it was merely his essence, I couldn't help but feel his tangible presence, touch, and love enveloping me in a gentle hold. In the darkness, he became a torch of comfort, reminding me that love surpasses physical boundaries and continues to thrive even beyond the veil of life.

His presence was a gift, a beautiful ray of light piercing through my grief's shadows. In those transcendent moments, I felt his love flooding my heart, filling the void left by his physical absence. The shared dance became a cherished connection that defied the limitations of space and time. In the embrace of the shadows, his spirit offered me solace and reassurance. It whispered words of encouragement, reminding me I was never truly alone. His love became a guiding light, leading me through the darkest corners of my pain and illuminating a path toward healing and inner strength. Through the dance in the shadows, I discovered love could transcend everything, even in the depths of grief.

It doesn't fade away; instead, it transforms into a source of comfort, a constant reminder of the beautiful moments shared and the lasting impact of a deep connection. And so, I continue to dance with him in the embrace of the shadows, finding solace in his presence and nourishing my soul with the love that transcends all barriers. It is a gift that reminds me there is light even in the darkest of times and that love never truly dies, for it dances eternally, forever guiding and cradling us through our struggles.

Nathan's life was a tapestry woven with threads of both hardship and resilience. At just 18 years old, he faced a brutal assault that left him with grievous injuries, including a metal plate in his frontal lobe. Despite enduring over twenty surgeries and untold suffering, Nathan's inner strength and beauty remained undimmed.

When we crossed paths, I was captivated by the man before me, unaware of his trials. Nathan grappled with chronic pain daily, often finding solace in the simplest moments. I held him close during his darkest hours, especially on rainy days when the pressure on his frontal lobe became unbearable.

Our union was a testament to love's resilience but was not without challenges. Nathan faced yet another brush with death, surviving another near-fatal brain surgery that threatened to tear us apart. Through it all, he remained steadfast, his spirit unyielding.

Tragically, Nathan's life was cut short by a senseless act of violence—a cruel twist of fate that stole him from me too soon. His passing shattered my world. But through the pain and loss, I have found strength. Though our time together was brief, our love was profound and sacred. Nathan's memory lives on in our enduring bond, a reminder of love's power to transcend even the darkest days.

Overcoming Grief and Embracing Renewal

In the crucible of grief, I discovered the alchemy of transformation. Like a phoenix rising from the ashes, I emerged from the depths of despair, my spirit tempered by the flames of loss and reborn in the glow of renewal. At first, the pain was all-consuming, a relentless tide threatening to engulf me in its depths. But in the midst of my anguish, I began to uncover hidden reserves of strength buried deep within my soul. With each passing day, I found solace in the simple act of putting one foot in front of the other, a testament to the resilience of the human spirit.

As I journeyed through the labyrinth of my grief, I discovered that healing is not a linear path, but rather a winding road fraught with twists and turns. There were moments when I stumbled, when the weight of my sorrow threatened to drag me back into the darkness. But with each setback, I learned to extend a gentle hand to myself, offering compassion and forgiveness instead of self-condemnation.

Slowly but surely, I began to cultivate a sense of acceptance, embracing the ebb and flow of my emotions with an open heart. I allowed myself to feel the full spectrum of human experience—the sorrow, the anger, the longing—knowing that each emotion was a stepping stone on the path to wholeness. In the fires of mourning, I forged a deeper connection to myself and those around me. I learned to cherish the moments of joy with a newfound reverence, knowing they were all the more precious for having been born from the ashes of sorrow.

Standing on the threshold of a new chapter in my life, I do so with a sense of gratitude for the journey that has brought me to this moment. Though the scars of my grief may never fully fade, they serve as a reminder of the strength that resides within me, a guiding light of hope moving me forward into the unknown. I am not defined by the losses I have endured, but rather by the courage I have faced them. Moreover, with that courage, I find the promise of a brighter tomorrow, where past wounds are but a distant memory and the possibilities of the future stretch out before me like an open road.

The Cosmic Dance Destiny

In the depths of my grief, amidst the shattered fragments of my reality, I've grappled with the notion that we create our own reality and shape our own destinies. How could I, in my wildest dreams, fathom that I had authored the heart-wrenching loss of over ten beloved family members? The mere thought seemed inconceivable; a cruel jest played by fate.

Yet, as I traverse the winding paths of sorrow, I've unearthed a profound truth that transcends the bounds of mere existence. It's not about the events but the profound lessons they bestow upon our souls. In the crucible of despair, I've discovered that our reality is not solely forged by our actions but is intertwined with the cosmic dance of destiny.

The departure of my beloved granddaughter, Ava, at a mere three months old, softly murmured the delicate, fleeting essence of life, while my father's valiant struggle against cancer illuminated the unwavering strength of the human spirit. Each instance of loss, a poignant segment in life's overarching tale, has etched an enduring imprint upon my soul.

Amidst the tumultuous storms of grief, I've found solace in the sanctuary of my spirit, where faith intertwines with the mysteries of the universe. In the sacred silence of my being, I've glimpsed the interconnected threads of life's journey, weaving a symphony of love and loss.

The violent deaths of my brother and husband carved deep wounds in my heart, wounds that once seemed insurmountable. But through the tears and the pain, I've discovered a reservoir of strength within me, a resilience born from the depths of sorrow.

Though my heart once bore the scars of unimaginable pain, I stand today as a testament to the transformative power of healing. In the wake of these tragedies, I've received many gifts of the spirit—strength, compassion, and a deepened connection to the divine. No longer defined by my past, I have emerged from the shadows, embracing a newfound sense of peace and purpose.

The luminous legacy of those who have journeyed beyond the veil continues to guide me, their spirits shining brightly as beacons of hope amidst the darkness. In the fire of sorrow, I've learned that a boundless reservoir of grace and resilience exists even amidst the most profound tragedies. Through my journey of healing and transformation, I now stand as a source of light and inspiration for others, a living testament to the power of the human spirit to overcome even the greatest of adversities.

Navigating Through Grief's Depths

In the midst of my grief, I stumbled upon a profound passage from the writings of the esteemed Lebanese-American poet, Kahlil Gibran: "Out of suffering have emerged the strongest souls; the most massive characters are seared with scars."

These words resonated deeply within me, offering solace and understanding during my darkest moments. As I delved into Gibran's wisdom, I found validation for my experiences and realized that my struggles had forged within me a resilient spirit. Through his insight, I grasped the transformative power of suffering, recognizing that it shapes us into stronger, more compassionate beings despite the scars it may leave behind.

Overcoming grief is a deeply personal and transformative journey that manifests in unique ways for each individual. It is a sacred pilgrimage through the depths of sorrow and loss, where the soul undertakes a process of healing and restoration.

In grief's heartache, there exists an opportunity for profound inner transformation. Through the tender embrace of our emotions and the gentle unfurling of our vulnerabilities, we uncover the human spirit's remarkable resilience. In this journey, we are invited to navigate the terrain of grief with courage and grace.

As we traverse this sacred path, we discover that grief is not an adversary to be conquered, but a companion to be honored. It becomes a chrysalis from which we emerge with newfound depths of compassion, empathy, and wisdom. Through our grief, we learn to hold space for our pain, to honor the memories of our loved ones, and to envision a future illuminated by their enduring love and legacy.

The alchemy of overcoming grief lies in our capacity to integrate the loss into the tapestry of our lives. It is a process of honoring the past while creating space for new beginnings, finding solace in the interconnectedness of all beings, and allowing our hearts to mend while retaining the gentle imprints of our cherished memories.

We find wellsprings of comfort and guidance in the gentle embrace of community, spirituality, and self-awareness. Through acts of self-compassion, nurturing practices, and seeking the support of kindred souls, we discover the transformative power of communal healing and interconnectedness.

In traversing the landscape of grief, we unfold our wings of resilience, enlightenment, and compassion, stepping forward into the radiant embrace of new beginnings. We forever carry within us the enduring love and cherished memories of those we hold dear.

Sacred Comfort: Finding Peace Amidst Tragedy

In the quiet depths of night, a somber call shattered the tranquil silence as the moon cast its gentle glow upon the world. It was my mother, her voice trembling with worry and fear. My brother, Daniel, had been missing for days, and concern gnawed at our hearts like a relentless storm. Little did I know this call would herald the beginning of a journey through the darkest corridors of grief.

As the hours slipped by, anxiety coiled like tight knots in my stomach, a silent prayer for Daniel's safe return echoing incessantly in my mind. Then, in the depths of the night, the devastating news descended like a heavy blow—Daniel was no more, a casualty of a violent crime. Shock and disbelief seized me, tearing through the fabric of my reality like a violent tempest. I stumbled through the house, tears streaming down my cheeks, cries of anguish echoing off the walls.

Falling to my knees, I sought refuge in prayer, reaching out to the heavens for comfort in my hour of need. And it was there, in my despair, that I experienced a moment of divine intervention. A gentle and tender warmth wrapped around me like a comforting embrace, suffusing my soul with a peace I had never known.

In that sacred moment, I felt the presence of divine love surrounding me, tangible and undeniable. With trembling hands and a whispered plea, I asked for strength to endure the unfathomable pain. In response, an infinitely compassionate hand rested upon my shoulder—a touch that spoke volumes without uttering a word.

Raising my eyes, I beheld the faint outline of a radiant white robe, a symbol of purity and grace. It was then that I knew, with a certainty that transcended mortal understanding, that I was in the presence of Jesus Himself. His touch upon my head infused me with a sense of peace that surpassed all understanding—a profound blessing bestowed upon me by the Divine.

Since that transcendent encounter, a lasting sense of tranquility has graced my soul, carrying me through the tumultuous waves of grief. Though the ache of Daniel's absence lingers, I find comfort in the belief that he has found peace in realms beyond our own. This experience has become a guiding light in the darkness, a beacon of hope and comfort that illuminates my path through the winding journey of life and love.

I am deeply convinced that God, in His infinite wisdom, never burdens us with more than we can endure. Whenever we humbly seek solace, the Divine graciously intervenes to heal our wounds and lighten our burdens.

Echoes of Grace: Silent Whispers of the Divine

As I sat one day at a business conference, captivated by the words of a motivational speaker, I felt a gentle, divine presence nudging me to go home and see my family before embarking on my next business trip. Despite my initial plan to continue traveling from the conference, the whisper urged me to prioritize my loved ones.

Acting upon that inner voice, I promptly contacted my oldest daughter, Helena, and asked for the opportunity to spend time with our precious three-month-old granddaughter, Ava. Helena kindly brought Ava over to my home that very day. My mother was also present, adding to the warmth and joy of the occasion.

Together, we devoted ourselves to cherishing every moment with little Ava. We engaged in play, laughter filling the air. In a tender moment, my mother serenaded her with a soul-stirring lullaby titled, *I Am a Child of God.* Ava responded with the enchantment of her smile, as if understanding the song's significance.

However, the very next morning, my mother and I received the devastating news that our beautiful Ava had passed away in her sleep, believed to be a victim of sudden infant death syndrome (SIDS). The weight of this loss laid heavily upon me, but I also witnessed the profound grief of my grandson, Brandon. His darling companion, lovingly called "turtle," would no longer be by his side.

In the midst of our pain, we cherish the memories we shared with Ava, recognizing the fragility of life and the profound impact she had on our hearts. The journey of healing embraces not only our own grief but also the empathy we hold for our grandson. We mourn the loss of an innocent life while turning toward the resilience that helps us navigate our grief and find peace in the love and cherished memories we hold dear.

Temazcal Tears: Healing Amidst Grief's Embrace

I remember this day like it was yesterday. I was sitting in that steamy Mayan temazcal in Mexico City, feeling like I was drowning in sweat. Each drop seemed to carry away a piece of the pain I carried inside. It had only been a few months since my sweet granddaughter Ava left us, just as she began to bloom in this world. The ache in my heart was unbearable. My mind raced back to that fateful day three months earlier, when her untimely death shattered our lives. Ava, only three months old, was taken by SIDS, leaving us grasping at the emptiness she left behind.

The heat inside the temazcal intensified, and I could feel myself struggling to breathe. I pleaded with the Shaman to let me leave, to escape the suffocating heat. But his words cut through my desperation like a knife. "Stay," he said, his voice steady and calm. "It is your ego that wants to flee. Your spirit needs to stay and heal here and now, in this sacred ceremony of the Mayan temazcal."

The temazcal, I learned, was more than just a steam bath; it was a revered Mayan ritual for purification and healing. Within its earthen walls, the heat symbolized the challenges and trials of life, while the steam represented the release and cleansing of one's spirit. As the sweat poured from my pores, I began to understand that this intense heat was not just physical discomfort, but a metaphorical fire burning away the layers of grief that had consumed me.

With each drop of sweat, I felt a piece of my pain dissolve into the air, carried away by the sacred energy of the ceremony. The Shaman's words echoed in my mind, urging me to surrender to the process and trust in the Mayan people's ancient wisdom. And so, with every breath, I let go a little more, allowing the healing power of the temazcal to mend the shattered pieces of my heart.

Whispers of Miracles

In the middle of this journey of grief, I discovered that death doesn't just bring pain with it; sometimes, it gifts us with tiny miracles.

In my voyage through sorrow, I was blessed with a tiny miracle. In the depths of meditation, Ava came to me in a vision. She appeared radiant, adorned in a flowing white gown, standing in a lush green meadow. With gentle grace, she approached me, holding a metal box of intricate beauty in her hands. "Open it," she whispered, and inside lay a stunning crystal bracelet, each tiny gem reflecting the light like a thousand prisms.

Ava spoke softly, her words carrying the weight of eternity. "I must leave now," she said, "but when you need me, just touch the bracelet." The vision filled me with awe and wonder, and I knew in my heart that Ava's love transcended even the boundaries of life and death.

I shared this profound experience with my dear sister Rocio, who creates beautiful jewelry. To my astonishment, she surprised me with a crystal bracelet identical to the one from my vision. Tears filled my eyes as I embraced this precious gift, knowing Ava's presence lingered within its delicate design.

Since that day, I have worn the bracelet always, day and night, even bathing with it, feeling Ava's loving presence close to my heart. In moments of longing or uncertainty, I touch the bracelet and am enveloped in her comforting embrace.

Through this extraordinary gift, I've come to understand that death is not merely a tragedy; it holds unexpected blessings within it, if only we open our hearts to receive them. Ava's bracelet is more than just a piece of jewelry; it is a tangible reminder of the eternal bond between us, a beacon of hope and love that guides me through the darkest nights.

Sacred Echoes: A Soul's Journey Through Time

In the sacred realm where spirits soar,
Eternal whispers echo evermore.
A pilgrimage unfolds, divine and true,
A soul's journey, both old and new.

Through shadows deep, we find our light,
Guided by love in the cosmic night.
With grace as our guide, we journey on,
Transforming pain, until it's gone.

Life's losses fade in the sacred dance,
As souls transcend, in a cosmic trance.
In death's embrace, we find rebirth,
A timeless truth, beyond the Earth.

So let us honor those who've flown,
Their spirits dance and their love is shown.
In the sacred quest, we are one,
United in love, under the sun.
Gabriela D.

Beyond the Veil: Embracing the Eternal Journey of the Soul

In the fabric of existence, death is but a doorway—a threshold through which the soul embarks on its eternal journey, freed from the confines of the physical realm, and reunited with the boundless expanse of the divine. Though the departure of loved ones may leave us bereft and longing, it is important to remember that their essence endures, ever-present in the web of creation and woven into the very fabric of our souls.

Life after death is not an ending, but a new beginning—a continuation of the soul's evolution as it traverses the vast expanse of eternity. Just as a seed must first fall to the earth to sprout and grow, so must the soul shed its earthly form to ascend to higher realms of consciousness.

In the embrace of the divine, there is no pain, sorrow, or separation—only an infinite ocean of love and light in which all souls are reunited and all wounds are healed. It is a realm of pure bliss, where the limitations of time and space melt away, and the soul is free to explore the mysteries of creation with boundless curiosity and wonder.

Though we may grieve for those who have passed beyond the veil, it is important to remember that they are not truly gone, but merely transformed—transcending the physical body's limitations and ascending to higher planes of existence. They watch over us with love and compassion, guiding us on our own journeys of growth and self-discovery from the realms beyond.

In the face of loss, let us take solace in the knowledge that death is not the end but a transition—a sacred passage from one state of being to the next. As we honor the memory of those who have gone before us, let us take comfort in the eternal truth that love is the thread that binds us all together, uniting us in a tapestry of interconnectedness that transcends time and space.

In the eternal dance of life and death, there is no separation—only the infinite embrace of the divine, calling us home to the love from which we were born and to which we shall return. And in this knowledge, let us find hope and inspiration to live our lives with courage, compassion, and grace, knowing we are never truly alone, but always held in the loving embrace of the divine.

From Heartache to Hope: Navigating Life's Losses with Grace

Sadness, loss, and grief are profound aspects of life. They challenge us to delve deeper within ourselves and explore the spiritual dimensions of our existence. Navigating the loss of a loved one, a shattered relationship, or even the heartache of estranged connections with our children or parents involves a sacred process.

Firstly, we must honor our emotions and allow ourselves to fully experience the depths of our sorrow. By acknowledging and embracing our pain, we create space for healing to unfold. Through these moments of vulnerability, we can connect with our inner selves and the divine, seeking wisdom and guidance from the higher realms.

In our spiritual quest for healing, we can turn to practices like meditation, prayer, or contemplation. These sacred rituals allow us to commune with our spirit guides, ancestors, or a higher power. As we open ourselves to their wisdom and support, we can receive guidance and find the strength to continue our journey amidst the storm of emotions.

Additionally, nurturing connections with supportive communities or seeking refuge in sacred spaces can be beneficial. Engaging with like-minded friends who have experienced similar losses can provide comfort, understanding, and shared wisdom. Participating in rituals, ceremonies, or group meditations can deepen our connection to the spiritual realm and foster a sense of belonging and interconnectedness.

Furthermore, the process of healing requires us to embrace self-compassion and forgiveness. We must cultivate love and understanding for ourselves, allowing forgiveness to mend the wounds within our souls. Doing so creates room for growth and transformation, inviting light to permeate the darkness that grief can cast upon our lives.

Each person's healing journey is unique and shaped by personal beliefs, spirituality, and experiences. It is an ongoing process that unfolds at its own pace. By intertwining our spiritual practices, embracing our emotions, seeking guidance from the divine, and fostering connections with others, we traverse the path of healing, gradually illuminating our way toward acceptance, peace, and restoration of the spirit.

Embracing New Beginnings

In the quiet corners of my heartache, I discovered the transformative power of grace—a gentle force that guided me through the turbulent waters of loss and sorrow. As I navigated the jagged edges of grief, facing the departure of loved ones, the erosion of relationships, and the relentless onslaught of life's challenges, I found peace in the embrace of grace.

Each loss felt like a dagger to the soul, leaving behind wounds that seemed impossible to heal. Yet, in my anguish, I discovered a reservoir of resilience within me, a quiet strength that whispered hope even in the darkest nights.

I found inspiration in the stories of others who had walked similar paths—those who had weathered the storms of grief and emerged stronger on the other side. Their journeys were a guiding light in my darkest moments, reminding me that healing was possible, despite seemingly insurmountable odds.

I sought comfort in embracing the community and surrounding myself with loved ones who offered support, compassion, and understanding. Their presence became a lifeline, anchoring me to the present moment and reminding me that I was not alone in my pain.

I turned to practices of self-care and self-compassion, nurturing my body, mind, and spirit with kindness and gentleness. Whether through meditation, journaling, or simply taking a walk in nature, I found moments of peace and respite amidst the chaos of grief.

As I journeyed through the labyrinth of my grief, I began to see the world through new eyes—eyes softened by sorrow yet illuminated by hope. I found comfort in the small moments of beauty that punctuated the darkness—the warmth of the sun on my skin, the laughter of a friend, the gentle caress of a breeze.

As I emerged from the depths of despair, I did so with a heart filled with gratitude—for the lessons learned, the strength gained, and the beauty discovered in the midst of the storm. Though the scars of my grief may linger, they serve as a reminder of the journey I have traveled and the dignity that has carried me through.

I am not defined by the losses I have endured, but rather by the grace I have faced them. And in that grace, I find the promise of a brighter tomorrow—a tomorrow filled with hope, healing, and the boundless possibility of new beginnings.

"Our elevation must be the result of self-efforts and work of our own hands. No other human power can accomplish it. If we but determine it shall be so, it will be so."

~ Martin Delany

CHAPTER TEN

Elevating Your Life

By John Spender

Isn't it tempting to cruise through life, stick to the same old routine, work hard, collect paychecks, and then just die? I mean, it's comfortable, right? I won't blame you for sticking to your comfort zone because I've stayed there many times over the years. I was glued to my last landscaping business for years. The holidays were nice, and there were moments when I loved the work, but part of me still felt unfulfilled.

But does it have to be that way? You've got dreams to chase, passions to pursue, and a whole world out there waiting for you to make a mark. If you are too comfortable with something, it's time to move on or to expand your current role so it's more challenging and rewarding. There is a famous saying: "*Everything you ever wanted is sitting on the other side of your comfort zone.*" It's time to step out of this zone because nothing grows there.

I did not explore the other side of my comfort zone for years because I thought this was my destiny—this is all I am capable of achieving—a work-life balance that I was proud to live. After a while, though, it became all too easy and familiar.

Moreover, I was wrong. I was not incapable; I was just scared. What if I couldn't sustain myself? What should I do next? What if I fail? These insecurities kept me in the same old, same old. But here I am talking to you about elevating your life. It means I have said goodbye to this hectic world successfully.

But how? Did I win some lottery, or maybe I found a bag of cash in a dumpster? Ah, no, those things are reserved for Hollywood scripts. Then how did I manage to break free from that cycle? You know what's the most powerful part of your body? No, it's not a six-pack. Going within, asking your heart, and aligning with your imagination. Your heart carries all the power to take you from the lowest of lows to the highest of highs.

Your heart has this amazing ability to inspire your mind to conjure up entire worlds just through imagination. Heart correction and imagination are the secret sauce, the recipe for success. Imagination is a womb for the three E's: expectation, exploration, and evolution, which gives birth to the fourth E, elevation.

I will tackle the power of imagination later in this chapter and invite you to bring your heart, too.

Understanding the Concept of Elevating Your Life

Before I reveal the secrets of elevating your life, you must understand what elevation means here. Is it elevating your social class? From below the poverty line to the middle class, from the middle class to the rich, from the rich to the elite? Again, I won't blame you for thinking that way. Today, elevating your life is synonymous with elevating your lifestyle. I have certainly been caught in that trap.

As you advance in your career, you get rewarded with better perks: a fancier car, a nicer home, a bigger bank account, the latest phone, access to posh restaurants, and the chance to travel to exotic places.

We often spend much time chasing happiness through pleasure and success. However, we may not realize that each time we indulge in a certain pleasure, the joy we feel from it diminishes. Similarly, the happiness we get from reaching a new goal is often short-lived, leaving us always wanting more. This cycle traps us in a never-ending quest for happiness. The desires of life are often fleeting.

Even the most delightful experiences, like savoring a delicious cookie or listening to beautiful music, only bring momentary pleasure. As psychologist Houston Smith points out, these highs are temporary, making us question whether there's more to life than brief moments of happiness.

Today, the measure of our quality of life is often equated with material possessions and achievements. This narrow focus on pleasure and success often fails to elevate our lives spiritually. Elevating your life means becoming a better version of yourself, living a better life than you did before, and taking steps towards self-improvement and contentment.

I discovered life coaching by accident; remember how I said I was stuck in a rut with my landscaping business? Well, I came across a seminar company teaching investing strategies, and it felt right to check it out. One thing led to another, and before I knew it, I was joining a year-long coach-the-coach program; by the end, I'd be trained in NLP (neuro-linguistic programming) and a qualified coach.

The best part was that a select few would be chosen to coach clients from the company's seminars held nationwide with hundreds of people in attendance. I hired a manager and focused on bringing in new business and studying for my new career as a life coach. I was out of my comfort zone and living on the edge a little bit. I can still remember our first group coaching call, and I was so nervous I thought my heart would pop out of my chest.

Getting outside your comfort zone is like a muscle; it's easier to take it step by step rather than trying to lift a whole stack of weights at once. This is one of the major things I learned in the coaching program over thirteen years ago and has stuck with me ever since. To practice getting outside your comfort zone, you want to start small.

For example, try taking a different route to work. How about brushing your teeth with your non-dominant hand or eating at a restaurant other than your usual? This way, you are taking small steps outside your comfort zone, expanding your mindset, allowing any insecurities to surface, processing them, and integrating them on a micro level. Getting outside your comfort zone is one of the best ways I know to evolve who you are and elevate your life. Other ways are:

- Spending more time with your loved ones.
- Following your passion and purpose.
- Visiting the places you love.
- Finding passive income sources.
- Living your life according to your values.

Elevation does not mean solely upgrading your financial health. It's more about embracing change, doing something different, and exploring things that can evolve your life. If you want to live a life that you love, you have to find what you love and pursue it.

Imagination: A Gateway to Endless Possibilities

Ever notice how your dreams often mirror the thoughts you entertain before bed?

Yesterday, I was thinking about the documentary I've been making, and last night, I was dreaming about working on the film with an editor. This is common for many of us; our subconscious has the same wavelength as our to-do list.

The point is that dreams and imagination are related to life. Your thoughts, actions, and capabilities are interlinked, and what you think in your subconscious also impacts your real life. But you know what? Imagination is a double-edged sword. The best use of imagination is creativity, and the worst is anxiety.

Imagination is a gateway to creativity. It enables you to open new doors that no one else has before. Take, for example, the Wright brothers. People in the early 20th century thought we could never fly, but the Wright brothers went against this conventional wisdom and invented the first airplane. Many saw apples falling from the tree, but only Newton imagined there must be a science behind this fall. A small, poor kid told his classmates that he would become the best rapper in the world, and he became Kanye West.

There are hundreds of thousands of examples. But the point is to use your imagination in the right way. Negative thoughts won't take you to a positive life. The extent to which you can explore those possibilities often depends on your ability to harness the power of your imagination. It's like having a dormant superpower within you, waiting to be awakened.

Think of your imagination as a key that unlocks doors to new worlds, new experiences, and new versions of yourself. When you tap into it, you open yourself up to a realm of limitless potential. Suddenly, the barriers that once held you back begin to crumble, and you find yourself on the brink of something extraordinary. At this point, most of us get off track. Instead of going the right way, we detour down a negative path. The allure of staying the same (safe) is always strong, and our minds can fill with negativity when we try to make a change. This negativity takes a toll on our minds, spirits, and bodies.

Once, there was a prisoner who was given a "hand to death" punishment. A Russian scientist got approval to experiment on this prisoner. He approached the man and informed him that he would be bitten by a snake instead of hanged. The prisoner was shown a highly venomous snake. Then his eyes were covered, and two needles were pricked on the middle finger instead of the expected snake bite. The prisoner died instantly.

The post-mortem report revealed that he suffered from a heart attack, but a strange thing happened. The report identified the presence of some toxic substances in his blood, which is very similar to that of snake bite victims. His body created these toxins because his brain believed a snake had bitten him. This proves that positive and negative energy causes our bodies to release hormones and toxins accordingly.

This is the power of your mind and how your imagination can take you to a whole new world. When you take your imagination down a negative path, it impacts your attitude toward life. You lose self-esteem and confidence in your abilities, resulting in only "failure." It's up to you to decide whether you want to think like the Wright brothers, who will be remembered forever, or like that prisoner who lost his life just by a needle prick. The choice is yours!

The Significance of Self-Awareness in Personal Growth

If you want to take one thing from this chapter, it should be self-awareness.

But of course, you know yourself better than anyone else, so what's the point of self-awareness here? Certainly, you know who you are and what you do. Self-awareness means knowing why you do what you do. You know how you feel, but self-awareness means knowing why you feel that way.

Many of us go through life reacting to things, following our gut instincts without thinking about them. But psychology says we're not just slaves to our emotions and reactions. Instead, we're the ones who observe and experience those emotions. Basically, when we're self-aware, we can step back and recognize why we feel the way we do. Moreover, when we understand our feelings better, we can control them. It's going from just reacting to life to actively shaping it. This self-awareness will allow you to direct your imagination, design your dreams and passions, and elevate your life.

Why be self-aware? What does it have to do with elevating your life? Let's say you are tasked with upgrading a product, like Netz 2.0 or the ultimate hamburger. First, you've got to understand what makes the current version tick. What's inside it? What makes it special? What's great about it, and where could it be better? What do people rave about, and what's not so hot? You can start cooking up your shiny new version when you've nailed down all these details.

Same deal with you. If you're looking to grow and improve yourself, you've got to start with a clear picture of who you are. If a product can't be upgraded without clearly understanding the current version, how can you elevate yourself without introspecting your current version? When you dissect yourself, you get to know the weak spots holding you back. What are your strengths that you could amp up? Which habits keep dragging you into bad decision loops? What's the stuff that fires you up? Once you've established a solid grip on yourself, you can investigate the root causes of any issues and start fixing them. For example, you are unlikely to progress if you are in sales but your social skills are too weak. So, know where you stand and what your flaws, shortcomings, and the areas for improvement are.

Our fears usually point the way. If you know you are shy, introverted, and terrified of public speaking, a logical place to start is joining a public speaking group like Toastmasters to improve your confidence and raise your ability to deliver a speech to an audience or team meeting.

That's what I had to do after I became a coach. I needed to speak at events and share my story, which scared me half to death. I attended a weekend speaking workshop to learn the basics, completed an online course, and volunteered to teach NLP at Mission Australia in Sydney, which increased my confidence enough to speak at my own events and try out for training roles as an NLP trainer. I eventually landed a position in a US company based in Bali running NLP trainings in Southeast Asia. Our fears often lead to our passion and purpose. That has certainly been the case for me. Now, I'm a book publisher, writer, and documentary filmmaker.

Embarking on a Journey of Self-Improvement

Alright, let's get down to business. You believe in the power of imagination and have cultivated a healthy dose of self-awareness. Now what? Now, my friend, it's time to embark on a journey of self-improvement. A walk to your inner self leads you to recognize your weaknesses and flaws. Once you identify those flaws, it's time to eliminate, or at least lessen them.

But how do you improve yourself?

Find something you're interested in or good at, put in the effort, deal with the highs and lows, and be patient, and you'll see progress. This quote from Morgan Housel fits well for self-help, even though he's talking about finance: "*The finance industry focuses too much on the actions and not enough on the mental side of things when you're trying to take those actions.*"

When you take the first step towards self–improvement, you encounter a long list of challenges that will keep you on the right path.

Imagine you are riding an elephant. Due to the sheer size difference between you and the elephant, you can imagine how difficult it would be to control the elephant. Well-known psychologists and writers like Jonathan Haidt and Robert Greene often mention this comparison. They use it to illustrate the struggle between the part of our brain responsible for thoughtful, long-term planning and the older, instinctual part that reacts quickly and subconsciously. To make positive changes in your life, the person (representing conscious, rational thinking) must exert some control over the elephant (symbolizing our subconscious and impulsive tendencies). Needless to say, it's easier said than done.

Sure, there will be setbacks along the way. You'll stumble, fall, and doubt yourself more times than you can count. But if your imagination is strong, your confidence will grow. Once your confidence is high, you can remove any hurdle that gets in the way of your self-growth. Start with small steps first, and before you know it, you're walking at a brisk pace, then jogging and running.

Identifying and Breaking Detrimental Habits

We all have those pesky little behaviors that hold us back and keep us stuck in a rut. Whether it's procrastination, self-doubt, or negative self-talk, these habits can wreak havoc on our lives if left unchecked.

But being human, it’s natural to exhibit bad habits. I decided to improve my fitness, but could not resist the urge to eat sweets. I promised to submit the assignment on time, but procrastination overcame me. I took an oath to avoid negative self-talk, but at the first sign of pressure, I made a relapse. This isn't me; this is everyone, or maybe most of us. We want to improve our lives, chase our dreams, and live happily. But these detrimental habits are glued to us so tightly that letting go feels like tearing off a piece of our own flesh.

Let that flesh go. Sure, it might sting, you might bleed, and there might even be a scar, but the best thing about being biotic is that you get to heal quickly. Once you heal, the freedom you gain from shedding those destructive habits is worth the temporary pain. For example, when I transitioned from my landscaping business into coaching, speaking, and writing, the payoff was a new skill set and fulfillment.

Don't create room for self-doubt; you can break free from those habits and replace them with ones that align with the person you want to become. It starts with recognizing the habits that no longer serve you and acknowledging their impact on your life. Once you’ve identified those habits, it’s time to take action. Start small, set achievable goals, and gradually build momentum over time. Maybe it’s committing to a daily meditation to quiet your inner critic or implementing a morning routine to kickstart your day on the right foot. Whatever it is, you can do it. Keep your imagination consistent and solid, and let the magic begin.

Encouraging Continued Commitment to Personal Growth, Fulfillment, and Living Authentically

You've been motivated, right? But for how long? Can you make it to the next mealtime?

This is what challenges people the most. We do get motivated early, we do take the first step, and when we encounter a small hump, we run back at twice the speed we began with. The road to elevation is not straight, and it shouldn't be. Can you get to the roof without using stairs or an elevator? Then how do you expect to elevate your life without pushing your boundaries?

Personal growth is not a college degree you can earn in two or four years; it is a lifelong pursuit, a continuous journey of self-discovery and self-improvement. But I hear many people saying, "I tried but could not see the results." When you want to enjoy stargazing, what do you do? You climb the stairs to the rooftop, where you can have a bright, full view of the sky. But can you see the sky from the first step of the stairs? No.

Do you give up because you can't see the sky from the get-go? Of course not. You ascend, buoyed by the knowledge that you will eventually be beneath that starry canopy. Then why stop investing in personal growth because you can't see immediate returns? Like you were sure you would reach the rooftop using stairs, I want your imagination to be that strong. Just like you keep climbing the stairs, I want you to keep improving yourself until you meet your destination: a life of fulfillment and authenticity. I want you to have the most spectacular celestial view that outweighs all the efforts you put into climbing stairs.

As you venture forth, remember this: you can do more than what you are doing right now. You have within you the power to create the life you've always dreamed of, to overcome any obstacle, and to achieve any goal you set your mind to.

But it all starts with feeling the desires in your heart and adding a little imagination. Your mind's eye can conjure up pathways you've never tread before. When you start imagining what you want to accomplish or create, that's when the magic happens. It sets you on a path toward your goals. But remember, it takes grit and hustle to make those dreams a reality.

In the journey of elevating your life, you'll inevitably encounter naysayers who doubt your aspirations, dismissing them as mere daydreams or the musings of a mind gone astray. However, it's crucial to remain steadfast in your convictions, trusting the inner voice that guides you. Embrace the hurdles as opportunities for growth, knowing that each challenge overcome brings you closer to your goals. Believe unwaveringly in your abilities and the boundless potential of your imagination. Nurture your dreams with relentless dedication, for they hold the key to unlocking your fullest potential. Remember, amidst the uncertainties, the best chapters of your life are yet to unfold.

**"Elevate your energy,
elevate your experiences."**

~ Unknown

AUTHOR BIOGRAPHIES

Amita McBride

CHAPTER ONE

Amita McBride is a gifted intuitive pioneer who works with people, animals and the earth, helping to facilitate deep transformation and healing in all aspects of life.

She has a passion for creating the extraordinary, personally doing so through her own ongoing awakening. Amita created her Sacred Raw Mayan Cacao healing line, working with the grandmother plants to open, balance, and strengthen the body, mind, and spirit.

Amita's work is founded upon personal empowerment to one's path of the heart, helping people align with new paradigms of belief, joy and expansion. She bridges diverse similarities with life's interconnectedness through her visionary approach.

Amita assists in bringing deep re-alignment through all aspects of life, including intensely difficult challenges, grief, and loss.

Expanding awareness and opening into new ways of perceiving with quantum healing, she assists with re-aligning the channels of the body and mind from the Soul, the true self. Love and forgiveness are the way forward.

Amita has written two books: *My Horse, The Hummingbird and A Very Small Tiger* and *Have Animal Crackers, Will Travel,*" and is currently working on two more. In addition, she has the honor of being the author of two *A Journey of Riches* books.

Amita is a seeker, glassblower, writer, speaker, healer, teacher, bee guardian, and nature lover who lives in Montana.

For more information about her and her offerings, please visit her website: rideswithfire.com.

Colleen Sabol Olitsky

CHAPTER TWO

For the past twenty years, Dr. Colleen Olitsky has been a partner in a world-class dental office, Smile Stylist, and has always had a passion for serving others.

A lover of exercise and self-care, Colleen has learned so much over the last decade about nutrition and wellness and how to achieve optimal health while aging gracefully.

These passions have ignited a fire in her to assist others in improving not only their physical health but also their financial health and mindset. Colleen believes that she has discovered the vehicle to achieve all of that and more. She is a seven-figure earner in her industry. Happy, healthy, wealthy, and in love is her tagline, and she loves to help others learn to dream again and live their best lives!

Colleen enjoys spending time at the beach, working out, playing tennis, reading and writing, date nights, watching her kids play sports, and traveling.

She is the author of *The Naked Tooth: What Cometic Dentists Don't Want You to Know* and has contributed chapters to four *A Journey of Riches* books.

Colleen is married to her best friend, Dr. Jason Olitsky, and they reside in Ponte Vedra Beach, FL, with their children, Chase and Gabriella, yellow lab Maverick, and kitty cat Tucker.

You can reach her at:
colleen@smilestylist.com
904.631.4827
IG: @anotherdayascolleen

Rebecca Shannon

CHAPTER THREE

Rebecca is a Mother to three boys, a leadership and empowerment coach with her own private practice, and known for her trademark 'hot pink' branding.

She lives in North Kent, England, in a gorgeous townhouse on a tidal creek, with her sons, two cats, and with Avocets, Herons, and Egrets as her neighbors.

Rebecca has adopted a uniquely holistic approach to coaching. Underpinned by her philosophy that if your personal life is out of kilter, you'll never be able to show up at work and fulfil your true potential, she helps people with all aspects of their lives, from the intensely private to the published corporate goals.

Rebecca loves to sing, write and travel and is committed to forever learning and creating a life she loves full of purpose and passion.

Mindful, intuitive, and curious, Rebecca creates hot pink ripples in the world that sparkle and shine through her love and light.

Rebecca's website: www.complementcoaching.com

Rebecca's email: rebecca@complementcoaching.com

Rebecca's LinkedIn: https://www.linkedin.com/in/rebecca-shannon

Idaliz Romero

CHAPTER FOUR

Idaliz Romero was born in Puerto Rico and raised in New York. She has been focused on self-development and elevating her life and the lives of her family and those around her. Most of her career has been working with the community focusing on helping in any way she can.

Idaliz studied Criminal Justice which led her to an internship and full-time job at a youth shelter. This led her to a career in nonprofit organizations where she worked in different capacities, such as teaching conversational English to adults and immigrants, among other services. This is the work she loves doing the most.

She is a mother of two, a grandmother of two amazing girls and a beautiful boy who is not physically here but who is always with her. She resides in Florida, where she is now retired, but continues to focus on learning, self-development, and spiritual connection.

This is her second anthology book collaboration with John R. Spender. She is passionate about writing and sharing parts of her story. She is now working on her first solo book, which will be published in 2025.

Idaliz is dedicated to improving her health and living life to the fullest. Her dream is to write memoirs to share her experiences and inspire others. She is grateful for the opportunities she has been given and the people who have come into her life because they have added to her personal growth and elevated her life.

Alessandro Gavello

CHAPTER FIVE

Italy. Half a century ago, Alessandro was born.

Early practitioner of Martial Arts by choice, Circus & Theatre performer by passion, Artistic Director by skill, Teacher by nature, Actor by trade, Practitioner of Commedia dell'Arte based in South Australia by fate, Licensed NLP Coach Trainer by call.

Collecting experiences along the way has allowed him to almost discover eternal youth as he practices to live in the present in the most enjoyable way possible.

You will find him amusingly participating in life, as he enjoys laughter and teaching people how to direct change by design. His vision is to live in a world where people can live free of phobias, limiting beliefs, and judgment and capable of truly making free choices. His mission is personal freedom, and his purpose is the exploration, discovery, and pursuit of knowledge about how much more we are with respect to what we think we are as we keep learning and improving.

He now mentors people to achieve their own personal freedom both physically and mentally, personally and professionally, as they learn to change their health, wealth, and relationships on purpose.

Contact details:
alessandrogavello@yahoo.it
WhatsApp and Telegram: +61 432877627
https://linktr.ee/alessandrogavello

Lynn Hayward

CHAPTER SIX

Lynn Hayward, a Scottish-born artist and digital innovator, has been redefining the boundaries of her art and advocacy through her personal battle with Complex Regional Pain Syndrome (CRPS). Spanning four decades, her artistic evolution from hand-printed textiles in Zimbabwe to cutting-edge digital mediums in Perth, Australia, has been a testament to resilience and transformation.

Honored as a finalist in the 2004 "Scottish Women" exhibition at Edinburgh's National Portrait Gallery, Lynn's artistry spans continents and mediums. Her journey took a pivotal turn in 2020 with a CRPS diagnosis, steering her towards a unique synthesis of voice-typed writing and digital creation. This adaptation sparked the development of Creative Visual Assistant (CVA), a tailored version of ChatGPT, which aids in her digital artistry and the crafting of intricate coloring pages scheduled for future publication.

Lynn's diverse use of mediums—from the essence of Scottish landscapes to the innovative realms of digital art—reflects a resilient spirit that challenges the narrative of disability. Her #Hashtagpoetry integrates visual and textual narratives, adding a dynamic layer to her artistic expression.

As a #CreativeSolutionsThroughAdversity advocate, her work extends beyond the visual arts into the literary sphere, with each piece advocating for CRPS awareness and engaging audiences in a tactile and emotional experience.

Join Lynn Hayward on a transformative journey where art serves as therapy and a beacon of hope, illuminating the path through adversity with every color, line, and texture she places before the world.

Sharee Siva

CHAPTER SEVEN

Sharee Siva is a self-described theorist who is deeply curious about the paradoxical nature of being human!

She is an abstract painter, collage artist and sculptor. Her works explore abstract concepts such as ‘patterns’ of consciousness, ‘impermanence,’ ‘reflection,’ and 'language and their historical and cultural significance.’ Sharee’s work is often quirky in nature, connecting the everyday with the esoteric.

Writing is a recent addition to her creative passions, and she begins with the intention of making a positive difference in the lives of others. Her writing stems from the foundation of living from one's own personal truth, sharing her theories on topics such as love, relationships, adversity, purpose, consciousness, spirituality, and other aspects of life in action.

Sharee was born in Melbourne where she resides with her two daughters. Upon completing her VCE, she was awarded a scholarship to study a Bachelor of Business Systems at Monash

University, Clayton. Sharee then began a business career, first with IBM Global Services and then as a founding member of Omnivision Pty Ltd. Sharee still plays a small role in this company. Still, She prefers to spend her time following her creative passions.

Mariese B Vacalares

CHAPTER EIGHT

Mariese B. Vacalares was born in the City of Golden Friendship called Cagayan de Oro City, in the booming island of Mindanao, southern Philippines.

She is the youngest of two daughters to her loving parents, the late Salvador Yasay Vacalares and Vilma Bokingkito Vacalares.

She attended college at the University of the Philippines in Cebu and Diliman with a degree in Bachelor of Science in Biological Sciences. Mariese proceeded with a medical course at Cebu Doctors' College of Medicine but later pursued an alternative course on Homeopathy, energy medicine and other complementary healing modalities. She holds a Masters's Degree in Human Resource Development.

Inspired by a Fortune Magazine article, Mariese ventured into real estate brokerage as a licensed practitioner and into real property leasing and development. She operates a beach resort called Mar

Villa Beach working on developing facilities for a wellness and wholeness center, and a Business Development Service provider.

Mariese is a certified Yoga teacher, Theta Healer, and Quantum Breakthrough Coach and is working on other certifications as a leadership and transformational coach. Her mission is to empower other people's lives and lead them to the best version of themselves.

She's developing *Kai'yah* as an integrated lifestyle movement and *Kaya* as a development center in conjunction with her advocacies, a foundation for the helpless and hopeless and for social entrepreneurship to help alleviate poverty in the country.

Contact Mariese @ Phone+639176268095, Viber, WhatsApp

Gabriela D Delgadillo

CHAPTER NINE

With a foundation in business and a flair for creativity, Gabriela is a globally recognized artist and international business entrepreneur. She has lent her expertise to multi-million dollar enterprises in various roles, including Consultant, Vice President, and International Marketing Director.

As the visionary CEO and Founder of The Gaby Effect, Gabriela leads a digital creative powerhouse dedicated to crafting extraordinary art and innovative products. Among her creations is The Game of Enlightenment, a transformative and interactive extra-sensory board game and experience designed to spark personal growth and insight.

Gabriela's journey as an artist began under the guidance of Italian Renaissance Master Frank Covino in 2000. Inspired by classical masters of art and literature and the beauty of nature, her work reflects a deep appreciation for exceptional people and the world around her.

Beyond her artistic pursuits, Gabriela is a sought-after success coach and motivational speaker. Mentored by icons such as Og Mandino, Jim Rohn, Zig Ziglar, and NSA founder Cavett Roberts, she shares her wisdom with audiences, inspiring individuals to realize their full potential.

In addition to her artistic and entrepreneurial endeavors, Gabriela is an experienced art therapist who has worked in the mental health field. She also shares her expertise by teaching intuitive art classes, using creativity as a tool for healing and self-discovery.

Gabriela further serves as a transformational life coach, focusing on mind-body psychology specializing in empowering women to reach their full potential and tap into their inner Goddess and Divine Feminine presence.

Explore Gabriela's creative universe and unlock the transformative power of art at www.thegabyeffect.com.

John Spender

CHAPTER TEN

John Spender is a 37-time International Best-Selling co-author, who didn't learn how to read and write at a basic level until he was ten years old. He has since traveled to more than 70 countries, territories and started many businesses leading him to create the best-selling book series *A Journey Of Riches*. He is an Award-Winning International Speaker and Movie Maker.

John worked as an international NLP trainer and coached thousands of people from various backgrounds through many challenges. From the borderline homeless to wealthy individuals, he has helped many people to connect with their truth to create a life on their terms.

John's search for answers to living a fulfilling life has taken him to work with Native American Indians in the Hills of San Diego, to visit the forests of Madagascar, swim with humpback whales in Tonga, explore the Okavango Delta of Botswana and climb the Great Wall of China. He's traveled from Chile to Slovakia, Hungary to the Solomon Islands, the mountains of Italy and the streets of Mexico.

Everywhere his journey has taken him, John has discovered a hunger among people to find a new way to live, with a yearning for freedom of expression. His belief that everyone has a book in them was born.

He is now a writing coach, having worked with over 300 authors from 40 countries for the *A Journey of Riches* series http://ajourneyofriches.com/ and his publishing house, Motion Media International, publishes non-fiction books.

John also co-wrote and produced the movie documentary *Adversity* starring Jack Canfield, Rev. Micheal Bernard Beckwith, Dr. John Demartini and many more, coming soon in 2024. And you can bet there will be a best-selling book to follow!

"Do not apologize for your decision to elevate your thoughts, upgrade your standards, or separate yourself from those who interrupt your greatness."

~ Cara Alwill Leyba

AFTERWORD

I hope you enjoyed the shared heartfelt stories, wisdom, and vulnerability. Storytelling is the oldest form of communication, and I hope you feel inspired to take a step toward living a fulfilling life. Feel free to contact any of the authors in this book or the other books in this series.

The proceeds of this book will be used for social giving at Jewel Children's Home in Northeast Bali.

Other books in the series are...

Living the Paradigm of Kindness: A Journey of Riches, Book Thirty-Five https://www.amazon.com/dp/B0CSXF1FBV

Creating Resilience: A Journey of Riches, Book Thirty-Four https://www.amazon.com/dp/B0CNVRDY38

Discover Your Purpose: A Journey of Riches, Book Thirty-Three https://www.amazon.com/dp/B0CFDLWTCB

Live Your Passion: A Journey of Riches, Book Thirty-two https://www.amazon.com/Live-Your-Passion-Stories-Fulfilling-ebook/dp/B0C5QXMNRQ

Master Your Mindset: A Jour*ney of Riches*, Book Thirty-one https://mybook.to/MasterYourMindset

Transform Your Wounds into Wisdom: A Journey of Riches, Book Thirty https://www.amazon.com/dp/ B0BKTJ377N

Motivate Your Life: A Journey of Riches, Book Twenty-Nine
https://www.amazon.com/dp/B0BCXMF11P

Awaken to Your Inner Truth: A Journey of Riches, Book Twenty-Eight
https://www.amazon.com/dp/B09YLYMQ4H?geniuslink=true

Awaken to Your Inner Truth: A Journey of Riches, Book Twenty-Eight
https://www.amazon.com/dp/B09YLYMQ4H?geniuslink=true

The Power of Inspiration: A Journey of Riches, Book Twenty-Seven
http://mybook.to/ThePowerofInspiration

Messages from The Heart: A Journey of Riches, Book Twenty-Six
http://mybook.to/MessagesOfHeart

Abundant Living: A Journey of Riches, Book Twenty-Five
https://www.amazon.com/dp/B0963N6B2C

The Way of the Leader: A Journey of Riches, Book Twenty-Four
https://www.amazon.com/dp/1925919285

The Attitude of Gratitude: A Journey of Riches, Book Twenty-Three
https://www.amazon.com/dp/1925919269

Facing Your Fears: A Journey of Riches, Book Twenty-Two
https://www.amazon.com/dp/1925919218

Returning to Love: A Journey of Riches, Book Twenty-One
https://www.amazon.com/dp/B08C54M2RB

Develop Inner Strength: A Journey of Riches, Book Twenty
https://www.amazon.com/dp/1925919153

Building your Dreams: A Journey of Riches, Book Nineteen https://www.amazon.com/dp/B081KZCN5R

Liberate your Struggles: A Journey of Riches, Book Eighteen https://www.amazon.com/dp/1925919099

In Search of Happiness: A Journey of Riches, Book Seventeen https://www.amazon.com/dp/B07R8HMP3K

Tapping into Courage: A Journey of Riches, Book Sixteen https://www.amazon.com/dp/B07NDCY1KY

The Power Healing: A Journey of Riches, Book Fifteen https://www.amazon.com/dp/B07LGRJQ2S

The Way of the Entrepreneur: A Journey Of Riches, Book Fourteen https://www.amazon.com/dp/B07KNHYR8V

Discovering Love and Gratitude: A Journey Of Riches, Book Thirteen https://www.amazon.com/dp/B07H23Q6D1

Transformational Change: A Journey Of Riches, Book Twelve https://www.amazon.com/dp/B07FYHMQRS

Finding Inspiration: A Journey Of Riches, Book Eleven https://www.amazon.com/dp/B07F1LS1ZW

Building your Life from Rock Bottom: A Journey Of Riches, Book Ten https://www.amazon.com/dp/B07CZK155Z

Transformation Calling: A Journey Of Riches, Book Nine https://www.amazon.com/dp/B07BWQY9FB

Letting Go and Embracing the New: A Journey Of Riches, Book Eight https://www.amazon.com/dp/B079ZKT2C2

Making Empowering Choices: A Journey Of Riches, Book Seven https://www.amazon.com/Making-Empowering-Choices-Journey-Riches-ebook/dp/B078JXMK5V

The Benefit of Challenge: A Journey Of Riches, Book Six https://www.amazon.com/dp/B0778S2VBD

Personal Changes: A Journey Of Riches, Book Five https://www.amazon.com/dp/B075WCQM4N

Dealing with Changes in Life: A Journey Of Riches, Book Four https://www.amazon.com/dp/B0716RDKK7

Making Changes: A Journey Of Riches, Book Three https://www.amazon.com/dp/B01MYWNI5A

The Gift In Challenge: A Journey Of Riches, Book Two https://www.amazon.com/dp/B01GBEML4G

From Darkness into the Light: A Journey Of Riches, Book One https://www.amazon.com/dp/B018QMPHJW

Thank you to all the authors who have shared aspects of their lives, hoping to inspire others to live a bigger version of themselves.

I want to share a beautiful quote from Jim Rohan, "You can't complain and feel grateful at the same time." At any given moment, we can either feel like a victim of life or be connected and grateful for it. I hope this book helps you feel grateful and inspires you to pursue your dreams.

For more information about contributing to the series, visit http://ajourneyofriches.com/. Furthermore, if you enjoyed reading this book, we would appreciate your review on Amazon to help get our message out to even more readers.

Printed in Great Britain
by Amazon

46954137R00126